GOOD GRIEF!

58 Ways to Manage YOUR Life

GOOD GRIEF!
58 Ways to Manage YOUR Life

by

Ruth Marcus

published by

Wide Awake
PUBLISHING
Sequim, WA

GOOD GRIEF!
FIFTY-EIGHT WAYS TO MANAGE YOUR LIFE

Copyright 2020 by Ruth Marcus
All Rights Reserved
Printed in the United States of America

Published by
Wide Awake Publishing
240 S. Sunnyside Ave. Unit 3007 • Sequim Washington 98382
wideawakepublishing.com

ISBN 978-0-9766004-7-3 (paperback)

Text in Adobe Garamond

No part of this publication may be reproduced or transmitted in any form,
or by any means, electronic or mechanical, including photocopy or recording,
or any information storage or retrieval system, without permission of the author.

DEDICATION

Without a readership,
a columnist does not retain her space
in a newspaper.

Thank you to all
who read my two columns,
Good Grief* and *Your New Life**,
during 2003 and 2010.

And, to new readers,
I hope you find a "nugget" here and there
that will help you manage your life.

•

*The original columns were published in the *Sequim Gazette* and *Living on the Peninsula*.

CONTENTS

Acknowledgements	xi
Court's in Session, Here Comes the Judge	1
Impatience: The Imperfection of Others	3
A Reason for Grieving.	6
Encouraging Words	9
Trust and Forgiveness: 101	12
Laugh Alot	16
No More Excuses	21
Lighten Up	24
The Art of Letting Go.	27
For Crying Out Loud	30
Life After Fifty: A Second Chance. . . .	33
Mad Scientists in a Mad, Mad World . .	38
Under the Bridge	43
Remove the Clutter	47
Do We Ever Graduate.	49
The Philosopher's Grocery Cart: Food for Thought	52
Turning Ouch into "Yes, Thank You" . .	56
Time to Make a Doggone Resolution . .	59
Living with Uncertainty	62

Willfulness and Willingness	64
Cultivate Gratitude	67
Life Soup and Crusty Bread	70
Pause and Effect, Take Your Time	73
Connoisseur of Fine Whines	76
Shall We Dance?	79
Knowing When to Say No	81
Mental Frequencies	84
Appreciate the Small Things	87
Two Simple Words: Thank You	90
Your New Life, Retired	92
How Do Our Gardens Grow?	96
Flossing Your Mind	99
Clear a Path, Remove the Clutter	102
The Greatest Show on Earth	105
Mental Plumbing	108
Great Teachers and Life Lessons	113
What Do You Call Home?	118
Sticks and Stones and Words	121
What's Love Got to Do With It?	124
Awfulizer or Energizer	126
Laugh More!	129
Your Heart is Not a Commodity	132

Hello? Are You There?	135
Love Sick	137
Compassion in a Heartbeat	140
Walk Your Talk	143
The Art of Weighing and Measuring	146
What a Day!	149
Forgiveness: It's About Your Well-being	152
What's Your Intention	155
Self-Talk: The Key to Feeling Terrific	158
Practice Gratitude	160
Autumn's Lesson: Impermanence	163
What's with the Vibes	168
Don't Fall into the Hole	171
Becoming Your Own Best Friend	174
Holy Dung	177
A Time for Thanks	179

ACKNOWLEDGEMENTS

I am especially grateful for the invitation and opportunity to have been a columnist for the *Sequim Gazette* and *Living on the Peninsula* between 2003 and 2010. My columns were titled "Good Grief" and "Your New Life."

Special thanks to...

SUE ELLEN RIESAU
former publisher of the *Sequim Gazette*
who offered me the opportunity

DIANA SOMERVILLE
friend and editor who nudged and put up with me for seven years

JUDITH DUNCAN, TEYA PRIEST JOHNSTON,
DONNA DOWNES, AND HEIDI HANSEN
who provided writerly support and encouragement.

NINA, ADRIENNE, DAVID, MARY AND SHARON
for their feedback in making a final decision
on a never-ending cover design!

RUTH MARCUS

Note: Some of the original essays have been updated for this printing.

COURT'S IN SESSION: HERE COMES THE JUDGE

LADIES AND LORDS OF THE COURT, PLEASE RISE.

The door opens. In walks an unending stream of judges, one after another. The faces look familiar. Hmmm…It's you. It's me. It's my brother's uncle and my sister's cousin. It's the whole human family, filing in, holding court.

What a conundrum! Judges spill out of the doorways and windows, into the streets. A packed courtroom. Everyone accuses and defends themselves: I'm the judge. No, I'm the judge. Who is the witness? What's the verdict.

And so it goes in Judgeville—in your house, in your face, in the most common place. You're late for dinner. You lied. Said it's up and I know it's down. I say it's you and you say, who? I run amuck and you say schmuck.

Silly how much time we spend being the judge. The list grows longer as we judge ourselves: I'm a thoughtless idiot. I'm lazy. I'm forgetful, unkind—even hypocritical. Too fat, too skinny, too strict, too lenient.

Court's in session. Too many judges. Endless cases. The backlog becomes a logjam of pointing fingers and accusations. Demanding rights, yet no amends. Case closed.

Consider the effect this judging has on you, on me, for she and he. No wonder we worry. No wonder we're anxious. It's plain to see we are all judges.

We judge Jack and Jill who live on the hill. We judge Miss Muffet who sits on her tuffet, criticize The Engine that Could, saying he never would. It goes on and on and on.

Whew! Isn't it easier to stop judging, fudging, and nudging—cooperate instead? I am you and you are me—the good, the bad and the ugly. Will you play, will you say, I made a mistake the other day? I stretched the truth. I don't have the answers, nor do you. Ladies and gentlemen of the court, let's take a recess. Recess, did you say?

You mean we will play? Who remembers how? Where is the joy mobile? Hand out balloons and share cartoons. Whistle while you work. Crumple the paper scribed Know It All. Apply yourself—stand tall.

What fun. A case of mistaken identity. We thought we lived in the land of Judge Judy. Then the blind mice show up, and we realize not one of us can see. We think we're smart, but we aren't. We pretend, argue and make a case, most of it is hot air.

Who knows anything for certain? Just when you decide you've got it, someone comes along and says, "you don't know what you're talking about."

I set out to prove I'm right. Judge Judy shows up in my living room and teaches me how to build a case. Voila! I've become a judge. A way of life—judge, judge, judge.

Stop! No more self-judgment. No more judging your neighbor. Let yourself be. Let others be. Listen to the Beatles, "Whisper words of wisdom, let it be, let it be."

■

IMPATIENCE...
THE IMPERFECTION OF OTHERS

HOW OFTEN DO YOU FIND YOURSELF IMPATIENT? Count the ways. Hurry. Stop repeating yourself; get to the point. Why didn't you fill the gas tank before we left? Must you text someone, then apply lipstick and grin in the rear-view mirror before you give up your parking space?

Impatience begins with annoyance and agitation. It walks hand in hand with self-centeredness: I want something changed. I want it changed now. And, I want it my way. Impatience is the rise of an internal fire that can become a volcanic eruption.

An example of impatience turned tragic was an accident involving two freeway commuters. A CEO tailgated a young SUV driver who was going the speed limit. Both were in the fast lane. The CEO's impatience grew hostile. He moved into the right lane and pulled alongside the SUV. Both drivers rolled down their windows and started fist shaking and shouting profanities.

Within seconds, the CEO veered in front of the SUV, causing that driver to lose control, jump a median and crash head-on into an oncoming semi-trailer truck. He and his wife died. Their five-month-old baby survived.

Two minutes of impatience and anger escalates. The lives of victims are changed forever. This is not an isolated incident. Unmanaged impatience causes reckless action—pain, damage, death and suffering every day. And, there IS a way around it. Each one of us can learn to manage our impatience.

Consider a scene at home. You want your children to hurry—it's time to head out for school and work. "Come on. Let's go," you shout as impatience escalates into anger.

One child comes running but not fast enough for you. Your impatience provokes a shouting match. You yell and swear. Your daughter yells back. Her eyes well with tears. The morning has turned sour for everyone. What can you do? Make a plan the night before. When it's time to leave, no drama.

Do you find yourself impatient with an elderly parent? You snap at your mother because she can't remember the details you think are important. Or, while caretaking your grandfather, you criticize him for wetting his pants for the second time that day. Impatience rears up in countless settings. It helps to be aware of special needs as we age—what to expect, what to plan for, how to manage.

At a busy restaurant, the waitress takes too long bringing you a menu. Your fingers tap the table. Your knee bobs enough to shake the floor. You scowl as she heads in your direction. By now, your stomach is churning. You promised you would not have a beer with lunch, but oh well, "It's the waitress' fault." Notice how quickly you blame others for your impatience and justify breaking abstinence.

I found myself impatient with a tech support person who spoke with a foreign accent. I wanted my problem solved fast and couldn't understand what he was saying. Taking a deep breath, I asked myself, "what's more important—haste or human relations?" How would I feel if I was learning a language and someone became impatient with me?

One thing about impatience is that it begins with me. When others are impatient, I have a choice how to respond. Like the tragic auto accident, impatience dueling impatience can turn deadly. Be aware of how easy it begins.

Notice when you are impatient with yourself: "Why can't I figure this out? What's taking me so long? How many times do I have to do this before I learn my lesson?"

Pressuring yourself is a wake-up call. It's an opportunity to slow down, take a deep breath—access a broader view of the situation. Will this matter tomorrow? A week from now? Ten years from now?

Instead of thumping fingers on the steering wheel, glaring as a shopper loads groceries into her cart—take a few deep breaths. Relax. The parking space isn't going anywhere. Change your attitude. Smile and forgive yourself for putting pressure on anyone. No one needs extra pressure.

How about carrying a fresh rose in the car? Take time to smell it instead of blasting your horn or shaking a fist. Calm yourself. Remind yourself that impatience increases blood pressure, distorts time and alters your ability to think clearly.

Instead of yelling, sing "row, row, row your boat, gently down the stream…merrily, merrily, merrily, merrily, life is but a dream." Then, smile. Make it a practice, an elixir that costs nothing and brings relief to you and others, even when managing impatience. Be gentle with others. Be gentle with yourself.

We all need more loving kindness.

A REASON FOR GRIEVING

DEATH KNOCKS. RELATIONSHIPS END. Life spins topsy-turvy. Loss and grief make challenging work. We resist, yet it is the heart's journey. Grieving lets us experience how connected we have been to a person, a pet, a job, a home, an idea—and so much more.

Grieving is a natural process that involves a range of emotion including shock and denial, pain and guilt, anger and frustration, depression, reflection, and loneliness.

The sadness comes in waves, sometimes powerful waves. We wonder if the all-consuming pain will ever end. Then, at some point, the darkness that engulfed us lifts. There is an upward turn, a gradual adjusting, and things seem to become calmer as the heaviness lifts.

Little by little, we accept a new future. Our hearts were broken, and the cracks are mending—we are forever marked by the experience.

This heart healing takes time. There is no right or wrong way to grieve. For example, two adult sisters who have been dealing with their mother's progressive disease for months, and engaged in round-the-clock caregiving, may feel tremendous relief when death comes.

Months of caregiving is exhausting. Death relieves the intensity of care and concern. For a while, the sisters seem relieved. Their bodies are catching up on sleep, muscles are relaxing, and the emotional stress of tracking medications, appointments, visitors and treatments has lifted.

Feeling relieved is a normal experience. After intensive care, relief is a healthy response. It takes time for the reality of death to set in and grieving to begin. It may take a month or more for a deep sense of loss to come to the surface. There is no shame in feeling relieved.

Grief is complicated. When young children are involved, the surviving parent faces challenges of single parenting. Not only is that person grieving the loss of a partner or spouse, but having to manage—alone—the children and the household. This can feel overwhelming.

It takes time to adjust. It's important for parents and children to work together, to talk about their needs. Children are often reluctant to talk about loss. It may bring up fear of losing the remaining parent.

Assurance and comfort, support and kindness help provide an atmosphere for families to experience their grief. Sharing stories, memories, laughter and tears are a part of the healing process. Everyone grieves differently. Some need to talk. Some need silence.

Reach out. Tell the school your child is grieving. Ask your church for emotional support. Turning to friends or a trusted counselor helps us grieve and receive support while adjusting to this major life change.

Rather than turn away from grief and escape in alcohol, drugs, or other activities that diminish your health, it's important to take care of yourself in nurturing ways.

Eat well, take naps, go for walks, talk with friends, work in the garden, sit by the river, join a grief support group. There are many simple ways of working with the grieving process.

Holding back tears bottles up emotions. This may cause physical symptoms: an aching heart, headaches, muscle aches and nervousness. Tears are part of our human experience. Let yourself cry. Let yourself be. There is no quick fix. Everyone has his or her own timing with grief. Sometimes grief comes in waves, out of the blue.

Relocating and retiring also activate grieving. Sadness and fear of the unknown is part of the process of saying farewell to a meaningful job, old friends, and a home you loved. You may feel lost, confused, sad, and lonely. You may question the meaning of life. Honor these feelings. Acknowledge you are going through a life transition. Grieving is a part of that process.

And, don't minimize the death of a pet or a special animal that feels like a best friend. Some of our closest relationships are with our beloved animal companions who bring us years of unconditional love.

We grieve when animals we love die. Some say, "get over it," but relationships with animals run deep. Honor your grief. Take your time.

There is a reason for grieving, and there is a season for all relationships. Everything ends. Take deep breaths and welcome the depth of your love. Allow your tears to fall. Grieving helps to acknowledge memories. The process heals a broken heart.

ENCOURAGING WORDS

HOME, HOME ON THE RANGE — when seldom is heard a discouraging word, what a difference it makes if we change.

Less discouragement and more encouragement benefits each one of us. Words of praise and appreciation heal relationships, improve the quality of life, and build self-confidence.

Remember when your son or daughter set out for the first time on bicycle training wheels—the sad scene of disappointment when they tumble to the ground? Instead of teasing or saying, "you're not ready to ride without training wheels," you were encouraging. Your son or daughter picked up the bicycle and tried again. Maybe you placed a helping hand on the seat to assist, but your action buoyed confidence.

When I reflect on the most powerful words that sustain me, four words come to mind: You can do it. When I feel discouraged and want to quit, or doubt my ability to make change, I remember my parents saying, "You can do it."

Have you heard the story about two frogs that fall into a deep pit. The frogs above gather and tell the fallen frogs they will never make it out. Both frogs jump with all their might.

Again, the frogs above tell them to quit. "You won't make it out," they croak. Then, one of the two frogs gives up and dies.

The other frog continues to jump while his companions above continue to yell, "Give up, give up." The frog in the pit makes one final leap, and he's free.

The other frogs ask, "Didn't you hear us telling you to quit?"

The relieved frog said he was hard of hearing. He thought they were encouraging him the entire time.

Think about it. The word encourage comes from the French word, le coeur, which means heart. Encouraging means putting one's heart into something, to add spirit and energy to one's efforts. Discourage is the opposite—to take away the heart's energy, to demoralize and disappoint.

I invite you to notice your thoughts and listen to the words you speak. Are they discouraging words? Or are they heartening to yourself and others?

How many fledgling artists, musicians or writers have had their spirits crushed by discouraging words from a teacher or a parent? What did you want to pursue and didn't because you were discouraged?

An old man approached the famous 19th-century poet and artist, Dante Gabriel Rosetti. The man showed him sketches and wanted to know if he had potential—would his work sell?

Rosetti looked at the sketches and knew there was little artistic talent. He told the old man as gently as possible that the drawings weren't very saleable. He was sorry but he didn't want to lie to him. The old man asked Rosetti if he would look at a few others done by a younger art student. Rosetti looked and said, "Oh, these are good. This student has great talent. These would sell for a fair amount of money."

Rosetti asked, "Who is this young artist?"

"It is me, 40 years ago. If only I had heard words of praise then, I would not have become discouraged and given up so soon." Words can impact an entire life.

When I was twenty, looking for work, a printer took me under his wing. He said, "I'll teach you a trade and you will never want for work in your life." His patience, generosity and willingness to pass along his knowledge and experience gave me skills I still use fifty years later. In fact, designing and publishing this book are demonstrations of the value of his patience.

He also inspired me to give back my knowledge and share what I've learned so that others can benefit. Every day, each one of us encourages and affects positive change. Simple words like: "That was a great dinner, Honey," or "Son, I appreciate the effort you are making to improve your grades," or "Thanks for being such a dear friend." Kind words strengthen relationships.

In the workplace, "You're doing a great job," are five words that make an enormous difference. And, plenty of thank you's encourage cooperation that grows.

Become an energizer—an encourager. At the end of the day, when the lights go out, give yourself the satisfaction that seldom was heard a discouraging word at your home—home on the range.

TRUST AND FORGIVENESS: 101

IN A SPLIT SECOND, THESE TWO WORDS can change your life. Trust and Forgiveness evoke deep emotion, imprinting your life forever.

Who have you trusted that broke your heart? What friend failed to honor confidentially? Has a business partner acted unethically? Did a parent encourage you to make a decision and it turned out to be an unwise decision?

What happens after trust is broken? Are you willing to forgive and trust again?

Psychiatrist Alfred Adler recommended, "Trust only movement. Life happens at the level of events, not of words." Thoreau said, "I think we may safely trust a good deal more than we do." And, Shakespeare advised, "Love all, trust a few."

What are your thoughts about trust? What makes a person trustworthy? Are you as trustworthy as you'd like to be? Trust provides the underpinning of all relationships and every transaction you enter. It impacts every area of your life.

Trust makes us vulnerable. Broken trust sets off internal alarms that can inhibit our willingness to trust again. When a glimmer of distrust or a shadow of doubt enters the picture, we curl up like a potato bug.

With trust, keeping your word seems to be the crux, yet actions, not words, show trust. When you don't show up, your words of promise become like cellophane—transparent. Others see through the words to your actions which are incongruent.

You promise your beloved, "until death do us part." Then comes a cheating spouse, or an unexpected death that shatters your sense of trust. You feel betrayed and wonder, "How could this happen?"

This question is not uncommon with broken trust. A trusted friend assured you that living on the Olympic Peninsula would be blissful. You packed up your life and left the freeway bottlenecks, the noise, and the fast pace of urban life.

Oops! Come to find out, Peninsula life is full of surprises: The well is drying up, the underground oil tank springs a leak, and your investments aren't providing what you had expected. How could these things happen when your trusted friend assured you that life on the Peninsula would be blissful?

Trust seems to have a hidden component. We venture into trust as if it were some mystical condition that insulates us from using our senses—including our ability to think things through.

Sometimes people trust with complete abandon: "What do I have to lose?" The next thing they know, they are shocked to loose nearly everything. How could this have happened?

When trust is broken, we want to hold that person accountable for the pain we experience. The degree to which we have invested trust shows up in the vocabulary we use to describe it. We describe our pain on a scale that ranges from frustrated to disappointed to betrayed to devastated.

It is not uncommon for people to want to "get even" or "pay back" the pain of broken trust—a sign of how challenging it is to manage the emotional response to betrayal.

Accountability, or admission of guilt, is what we want. We want the betrayer to fess up, confess, bow down, and pay penance. We repeat the story over and over like a broken record, each time concluding in despair, "I can't believe this happened!"

Shock and anger, grief and sadness are natural responses when we feel someone has betrayed our trust. But when we get stuck in a loop and fail to move on, it compromises our well-being.

What can we do to move through broken trust, and on to forgiveness? Will we trust again? Will we be able to forgive?

Is it possible that these stages are the "seasons" of the heart—a natural learning process that teaches us to love and appreciate more, or turns us into curmudgeons who refuse to trust anybody ever again?

To trust again requires facing the pain. New insight brings forgiveness and a willingness to move on.

Self-inquiry is a powerful tool to free us from suffering. With the care and tenderness of an archeologist unearthing a great "find," question yourself. Look deeper with an interest in understanding who you are and the reasons you trusted.

Sometimes we trust for our selfish benefit or because we need reassurance. We rush in "where fools fear to tread," acting with complete abandon. And, sometimes we trust our sexual appetite and forget that we have intelligence and values—both become compromised.

Ask yourself questions: What was I thinking when I trusted this person or this endeavor? Did I have my eyes wide open or was I wearing blinders? Were there telltale warning signs I ignored? Did I make up excuses to justify the relationship? Did I lie to myself because I feared the truth? If I had told myself the truth, what would be different? Was I avoiding confrontation at the expense of not expressing my needs and concerns? What part of this am I responsible for? And what have I learned that can make me a wiser person?

The process of self-inquiry is an act of love—a means of befriending yourself. By unearthing your own truth, you learn to trust yourself more. You notice small ways you betray yourself or minimize who you are. This process brings light to the shadows where doubt lives.

Notice when you undermine your integrity, compromise your values, and diminish your self-worth. Instead, free yourself from the burden of dishonesty, self-betrayal and self-doubt.

Self-inquiry is a gentle truth-telling process. It guides you to see and appreciate your humanness. It's a process of forgiving and being kind to yourself—nurturing and trusting yourself. In time, you find yourself with a compassionate heart—the antithesis of self-loathing.

Telling the truth is the path toward befriending yourself—your shortcomings and errors, your strengths and talents—a process of becoming more trusting and trustworthy.

Broken trust never "feels good," but rather than feel devastated, you realize everyone falls short at times. Learn to acknowledge the "ouch" and move on rather than spiral into resentment.

Forgiveness begins with willingness. To see things from a broad view, and admit your own errors, strengthens your ability to forgive others. The saying "there but for the grace of God go I" is an admission to our humanness.

To trust or not to trust? I offer the words of Cardinal de Retz (1614-1679), "A man who doesn't trust himself can never really trust anyone else." And that goes for a woman, too.

■

LAUGH A LOT

I WAS MAKING MY MONTHLY RUN to that big membership box store when I experienced one of those rare parking lot moments. Parked in the next space, a middle-aged man rolls down his car windows to make sure his dog has fresh air. The mixed-breed dog stretches out in the back seat. As the man leaves his car, he shakes his finger at the dog who is now standing, looking out the window. "Stay! I'll be right back. Stay!" He shakes his finger for emphasis and repeats, "Stay!"

Then another driver gets out of an adjacent car, scratches his head, focuses on the fellow who's giving the order to "stay," and says, "Man, just put your car in park."

I couldn't help myself. I burst out laughing. In that unexpected moment of spontaneous hilarity, I was reminded once again of how important it is to laugh. It feels so-o-o good. There's plenty of everyday humor around us if we are willing to be present, to listen, look and see the humor in any situation.

With all the challenges we face—the economy, ecosystems, healthcare, you-name-it—laughter provides relief.

One of my favorite humorists is Swami Beyondananda. He suggested we make changes by starting a new political party, the Right-To-Laugh Party, to encourage peoples of the world to laugh together instead of cry. I think he's onto something.

When surrounded by a sea of bad news, Swami reminds us not to use more energy than we have in reserve. "We cannot charge energy on our Ascended Master Card and repay it next lifetime." We must face our situation—face it with plenty of humor, then experience new ways of seeing that otherwise might seem overwhelming.

Take Swami's cue: "Appreciate why it took Buddha forever to vacuum his sofa. He had no attachments."

Whether it's a simple knock-knock joke based on puns or words misused or misunderstood, seeing the absurdity in every day situations not only feels good but is good for what ails us. Just as our bodies need us to walk every day, our mental health needs us to watch for everyday chances to grin and laugh.

You may recall the story of author Norman Cousins who overcame a serious chronic disease by laughing at his favorite comedy shows such as Candid Camera and Marx Brothers movies. He also hired a nurse to read funny stories to him—and found that ten minutes of hearty laughing could provide him two hours of pain-free relief. Soon he was off painkillers and other medications. Check out his book, Anatomy of an Illness, for more details on his laughing therapy.

Perhaps it's useful to ask, do we laugh because we are happy and healthy, or are we happy and healthy because we laugh? Let's take a closer look.

Laughter provides instant stress relief and an antidote to most suffering. Instead of spending millions on expensive prescription drugs, we would do well to consider using this built-in coping mechanism. Applying big doses of grins, giggles and laughter—instead of downing prescription cocktails—can eliminate all kinds of problems and leave us with many feel-good side effects.

Fifteen small muscles shape your face into a smile, increase the blood flow and bring a happy glow to your face when you laugh. Your mouth opens letting out those great ha-ha-ha's which increases your intake of oxygen in huge gulps. Laughter oxygenates all your organs, boosts your immune system by elevating health-enhancing hormones like endorphins while reducing stress hormones like cortisol and epinephrine. No wonder laughing gives you a general sense of well-being.

There's more. Laughter elevates your vocal response to infectious hysteria. Have you noticed how contagious it is? It also wrestles your vessels, causing the diaphragm muscles to pump down and up—a great workout. All that air exchange enriches your body's blood oxygen level. It's an inner trip to the gym without running two miles for a workout.

Think about it. The moment laughter bubbles up, irritations and resentments slip away. It has no negative side effects. Can you imagine an entire community enjoying laugh fests—everything from deep, belly-shaking laughter to giggles and smiles galore? That's what one person imagined in 1995.

Dr. Madan Kataria, a Bombay physician, believes that laughter is good for the heart and soul. Recognizing that laughter is a universal language with the potential of uniting humanity, he founded the International Laughter Club movement. Large groups of all ages gather as Dr. Kataria encourages participants to spread out their arms and laugh for no reason.

Reminders are everywhere. Santa ho-ho-ho's himself down the chimney. Alfred E. Neuman has that eternal grin. The Dalai Lama giggles his way to enlightenment and the Laughing Buddha is reminding you to laugh, laugh, laugh. Even the digital smiley-face icons remind us to put on a happy face. And LOL, an acronym for Laughing Out Loud, frequently appears in text messages and emails.

Humor tickles each of us in unique ways, and there's plenty to go around. Tap into it! You can jump start laughter by tickling your willing partner under the arms, ribs and under the neck. Giggling and wiggling are feel-good actions for body, mind and psyche.

A good laugh at your own expense is humbling, humanizing and entertaining. No need to take yourself so seriously.

When my granddaughter was barely three, I'd point to objects and ask, "What color is this?" She'd respond, and I praised her correct answers. It didn't take long before she turned my little efforts upside down. "Grammy, why don't you know your colors?" Ah, the gift of humor in the words of a child. I still laugh when I think about her comment.

I love the story of the heart surgeon waiting to talk with the service manager at a motorcycle repair shop. The mechanic, removing a cylinder head from a Harley engine, recognized the surgeon and called out, "Hey, Doc, look at this engine. I open its heart, take valves out, fix 'em, put 'em back in, and when I finish, it works just like new. How come I get a small salary and you get big bucks when we do the same work?"

The surgeon paused, smiled, leaned over and said, "Try doing it with the engine running."

Humor is so useful in treating people's illnesses that there are clowning programs to bring laughter and joy to bedsides. These programs train Clown Doctors to provide good humor services in hospitals, nursing homes and rehab centers.

No question, the more you laugh, the more you elevate everyone's mood. Laughing is a social activity—a great pastime to share with friends. Games like charades, bunco or croquet on the lawn create a light-hearted mood and bring joyful laughter.

Incorporate laughter into your daily routine. Watch 30 minutes of comedy each morning—reruns of *I Love Lucy, Friends,* or *Laurel & Hardy.* Watch feel-good films—*Groundhog Day, Little Miss Sunshine,* and *Oh Brother, Where Art Thou?* Listen to audio recordings of your favorite stand-up comedians as you commute to work.

You'll find hilarity in your local newspapers and the Sunday church bulletins, too. I enjoy humorous errors and typos: "Thursday night, potluck supper. Prayer and medication to follow." Or, "A bean supper will be held on Tuesday evening in the church hall. Music will follow." I especially like these two: "Low Self Esteem Support Group will meet Thursday. Please use the back door." And, "The new tithing campaign slogan: I Upped My Pledge. Up Yours."

When you find yourself too serious and want more laughter in your life, spend more time with kids—yours or a friend's, or better yet, your grandkids. An average six-year-old laughs 300 times a day while an adult laughs only 15 to 100 times.

Don't fear being spontaneous and silly. Prepare yourself with humor tools—cartoons, jokes, signs and props. Rubber chickens, anyone? Or how about a whoopee cushion or Groucho Marx glasses, complete with nose and mustache? Have fun. Whistle a happy tune. Take up clowning. Or, make-up silly songs to suit a special occasion. Put on a wig and surprise your friends with your new image.

Imagine a kindergarten class on the ferry to Seattle singing "row, row, ho-ho-ho; gently down the stream; giggly, wiggly, sniggly hee; happy all are we." Laughter is the best medicine. Go ahead—laugh. Laugh a lot!

NO MORE EXCUSES

MY EXCUSE? "I HAVE NO WILLPOWER."

The truth? "I need to practice self-control."

And you? What are your excuses? Too many things to do? Or, is "yes" an automatic response?

Excuses are a means to opt out. They are untruths that diminish your abilities, your responsibilities and your presence. They are you playing small in a world where we benefit by fully participating.

Marianne Williamson wrote, "Our deepest fear is not that we are inadequate; our deepest fear is that we are powerful beyond measure."

I invite you to face your excuses, see how they limit your life. Words of fear like can't, too difficult, not smart enough, and I don't know how are obstacles between integrity and responsible action.

"I'm the victim of lousy luck." Luck is what you pull out of your back pocket—an excuse you use when you are unhappy with what's happening. Your phone bill says you have a five-dollar late fee. Is it lousy luck, or was your phone service disconnected because you mailed your check after the due date?

Consider this: No more excuses. If your throat tightens and your gut gets jittery with this proposition, is it a sign of leaving your comfort zone—the zone of avoidance and untruths?

"I love things the way they are." Ah yes, the crème de le crème of excuses. From financial systems to environmental standards to healthcare models, we love to support the status quo. Same-O, Same-O feels cozy and familiar.

"If it isn't broke, don't fix it"—an excuse that numbs creativity. Imagine, instead, encouraging your children to explore and experiment. Imagine removing your half-witted excuses, "I can't make a living doing that." Or, "It's a waste of time." Or, "People will think I'm crazy."

Notice your behavior. Begin today. Ask yourself, "What excuse is preventing me from taking action? What do I fear?" Notice the propensity to retreat. To blame it on someone else: "Opportunities knock at her door, not mine." Resentment grows weeds when we fertilize life with excuses.

If you say, "I don't have enough money and I'm not smart enough," consider Apple's iconic Steve Jobs. He dropped out of Reed College when he couldn't pay the tuition. That didn't stop him from pursuing his passion—a passion that turned into a potential of supporting nearly 40,000 students at Reed College for four years.

Ralph Lauren was a college dropout, too. And novelist J.K. Rowling was on welfare raising her daughter when she got word that Bloomsbury agreed to publish her Harry Potter book.

Cut out excuses—"I'm broke. I'm no genius. I'm jinxed."

Yes, terrible things happen in life. Ask Oprah. She overcame endless obstacles and didn't let terrible things hold her back.

No more excuses. End the litany: "He hit me first. She made me do it. Everybody else is doing it."

Imagine taking the energy devoted to excuses and turn it into responsible solutions. Admit your errors. View them as positive contributions. Become a listener, an encourager—learn, grow, and forgive instead of blame and shame.

Give up small excuses. Instead of saying, "I couldn't get here on time," tell the truth, "I'm sorry. I spent too much time puttering.

Please forgive me."

Be willing to let go of self-righteous excuses: "I'm entitled to act this way because ____." How many of you wallow in toxic self-pity for endless reasons? Every excuse holds you back from your greatness.

We long to belong, yet we make up excuses that express our fears. I don't fit in. I'm not good enough. I'm untrustworthy.

No more excuses! Become active, honest and contribute to the well-being of this great human family.

Thomas Edison didn't make up excuses. With over 5000 attempts to invent the light bulb, he acknowledged each experiment as a valuable step toward the solution.

Next time you want to make up an excuse, remember Thomas Edison's tenacity to pursue his dream with boldness. Turn off the excuses. Turn on your inner light. The world needs your brilliance—NOW. No more excuses.

■

LIGHTEN UP

ALTHOUGH I HAVEN'T WATCHED television for years, I do read online newspapers, magazines and discuss current events with friends. I hear plenty of doom and gloom, bickering, blaming and things that need fixing. It's easy to get pulled in, but I need not become part of the doom and gloom.

I have options, and so do you. Remember that song, "Let the Sun Shine In"? It's a catchy little reminder: Where you direct your attention is how you experience life.

When you focus on doom and gloom, you slip into a slump—get depressed. When focused on things that bring you joy, your spirits improve. Hum and sing, "Don't worry, be happy."

Focus on the stuff that's not working, and yes, you feel overwhelmed and stressed. I'm not suggesting that you bury your head in the sand, or, that you deny broken things that need attention. I suggest you put emphasis on the things that are going well, things that energize you, and things that lift you up.

This past summer, I took an Alaskan cruise with my 11-year-old granddaughter. At the entrance to the family dining room, there were crew members greeting us with big smiles. To every person who walked through the door, they said, "Happy, happy, smiley, smiley." I couldn't help but smile every time I entered.

It intrigued me. After three days, I asked a greeter if he did that on his own volition or did management tell him to say "Happy,

happy, smiley, smiley." He nodded, "Yes, management requested the greeting."

I asked if he knew why. With a smile on his face, he said, "Most people are mildly depressed, and we want to encourage them to smile, enjoy the cruise, have fun—enjoy life."

How's that for pointing people in a positive direction? I loved the simplicity of the greeting—so much that I have continued saying it ever since. It's a simple reminder to change course when doom and gloom have a grip on my family, friends and me.

Turning your attention to the positive is one of those life choices you get to make (or not). A cheerful reminder of making positive choices comes from my 92-year-old friend who lives in a retirement community where many residents avoid "organ concerts"—the ritual of complaining about every ailing organ. Some answer the familiar "How are you?" with "Any day on this side of the grass is a good day."

Next time someone laments about everything that's going wrong in the world, notice what happens to your energy. Here's a chance to lift yourself up. Lighten up. Change the topic.

Better yet, encourage the purveyor of doom and gloom to talk about creative solutions and innovative change. The two of you will feel energized by sharing new ideas.

How do you get to "Happy, happy, smiley, smiley?"

Let go of the need to be right. Voila! No one ends up feeling wrong or blamed.

Let go of wanting things to be perfect. Nature is not perfect. Yet, beauty is within bare-branched trees, flowering weeds and blustery winds.

Let go of nagging. Praise and say "thank you."

Take a moment to remember that no one is perfect. It's a relief when you recognize we're all in this together—shortcomings, foibles, frailties and all. Lighten up. Laugh more.

What goofy little thing do you find endearing in someone you love? What silly little thing do you like about yourself? Experiment with different ways to respond to internal critical voices. For example, "Everyday, in every way, I love and accept myself completely." Or, "Hey, I'm human. I'm willing to do my best." Or, "Another learning experience!"

Remember to nurture yourself. Eat well. Exercise. Take a class. Express your feelings. Ask for help. Do something kind for another person every day. Celebrate small successes—yours and others. Give hugs. Appreciate waking up in the morning and give thanks at the end of the day.

And, when people get you down, spend time in nature. Hike, bike, and bask in the wonder of trees and rivers, migrating birds and falling leaves. Breathe the fresh air. Fill yourself with beauty. Lighten up.

Happy, happy, smiley, smiley!

THE ART OF LETTING GO

DECIDUOUS TREES OFFER us one of nature's most important lessons—the art of letting go. There is a season for everything. Why do we hang on to outdated beliefs? Why do we stay in unsatisfying jobs and relationships?

To let go means change. For most of us that requires a risk of the unknown and courage to move forward. It is an emotional experience. With deep attachments to people and belongings, you might wail, "No-o-o-o-o-o." Other times, you let go with a sigh of relief.

Muscles tighten and release. Observe the sensations of a frown versus a smile. Are you tight-fisted or generous of heart? Do you hold a grudge or forgive with ease and grace?

Remember the first nick in your shiny new car? "Not my car! How could this happen?" Consider the guilty party and your blood pressure rises.

Little did you realize how attached you were to that new car. You stewed for days while your partner attempted to calm you. "Let it go, Honey, it's just a car." Every word of encouragement made you resist accepting it was an accident. Did it take a week, or a month, before you realized that stewing accomplished nothing except acid stomach and headaches?

We lose favorite things—sweaters, gloves, a piece of jewelry, electronic devices. Do you accept the transitory nature of life? How long before you let go?

Many people walk around for years focused on things that happened five, ten, twenty years ago, refusing to let go. The web of justifications for anger and pain create more anger and pain. How much energy do you spend proving you are right?

What happened years ago, or even five minutes ago is history. Take responsibility. Living in the past is a waste of precious current time. The past was Then. Now is Now.

Yes, most of us cling now and then, but consider the belief and move forward. Ask yourself "what is the source of this belief"? Is it one you learned from someone else? It's common to share the same beliefs as your parents, but do you ask why? Are your beliefs based on keeping the peace?

Spouses often defer to a spouse to avoid conflict. Examine your beliefs. You might be surprised what you discover. Elimination of outdated beliefs is humbling. You can admit your humanness—find relief in letting go.

Every leaf on a deciduous tree lets go. Life is endlessly letting go, yet we live with expectations. We expect the sun to rise and set. Water will come from the tap and grocery stores will have food on the shelves. Most of us have expectations of family and friends, neighbors and nations.

When a water pipe breaks or a trucking strike plays havoc with everyday supplies, we are shaken. Our attachment to necessities and the inherent comfort level they provide make a difference. Preparedness for these situations includes acknowledgement and willingness to do with less.

When family and friends disappoint you, notice your need to control your universe. "Why bring up that subject" shows uncomfortable feelings. Practice taking a deep inhale and a deep exhale—a useful tool for a more thoughtful response.

Life's biggest letting-go-lesson is death. Do you share your concerns and beliefs? Do you prepare for the inevitable? Our culture avoids discussing death and dying. Our focus is on eternal youth (face lifts, tummy tucks) and longevity (medical gadgets, procedures, pharmaceuticals, transplants and implants). Longevity may not improve quality of life, yet we go to great lengths to sustain it. We consider it a better choice than facing death. Imagine death as important as birth. We come and we go. Joy and grief, the same coin as life and death. Examine the connection, become fear-less.

Are you steeped in religious practices that focus on a glorious life after death? Or, is karma and eternal life your view? Others espouse the belief that death is nothing more than the decomposition of the body.

We might do well to appreciate the art of letting go. Savor what is and what was. Express gratitude for time spent on earth. Thank your friends and family. Be grateful and let go.

FOR CRYING OUT LOUD

WE ARE CRIERS—all of us. We were from the beginning.

Remember your first cry? That forgotten experience of being squeezed through the birth canal and finding yourself in a bright, cold environment. Most of us let out a wail, and if we didn't, the doctor or midwife made sure we did.

Was it a scream of "OMG, what am I doing here?"—or a spontaneous expression of joyful gratitude for having completed a dramatic and traumatic entry?

Crying continued. Cry, and diapers are changed. Cry, and someone feeds us. If we were fortunate, crying in the middle of the night brought someone to cuddle and comfort us, and rock us back to sleep. Crying works. A simple language, as effective as our sweet baby smile.

When we became toddlers, we still cried, but were taught to use words instead of tears. Some of us resisted and got a reputation of being the out-of-control-kid, the one wailing in the shopping cart—the "I want it" tantrum.

We learned if we wailed loud enough, mother gave in and provided whatever we desired, or someone hurried us out the door. Getting our way by crying depended on how smart, determined and consistent our parents were.

Once we started school, peer pressure entered the equation. If someone called us a cry baby, it didn't take long to give up the crying.

Most of us learned that big girls don't cry, and depending on your culture and family-of-origin, we know that boys who cry are unmanly. "Suck it up; get a grip." An emotional handicap.

The only time I saw my father cry was when I was in the sixth grade. He sobbed at my grandmother's funeral. I'll never forget that day. I only saw him cry one other time—when he got laid off from his job. The company was closing the local plant. He had a wife and four children to feed.

Most people prefer to laugh than to cry, but sometimes we laugh until we cry, and other times we cry until we laugh. Tears punctuate important moments in our lives.

Friends cry tears of joy when reunited after years of being apart. Fathers show tears when giving daughters away in marriage. The whole family cries when sons and daughters go off to war. And, we cry tears of relief when they come home.

We cry when we're scared. Consider the teenage driver who backs into your car. The damage is minor, but tears are not uncommon. It's a release of mixed emotions. She worries her insurance rates will skyrocket and what-are-my-parents-going-to-say?

Tears become sobs when emotions overwhelm us. We gasp and choke. As one wise teacher said, "Tears happen when your heart cracks open." We long to express the full range of human emotions.

Often we blubber through tears, a difficult time accepting unexpected generosity and kindness. Tenderness finds its way to the surface and a fountain of tears follow.

Many of us become confused along the way. We hesitate to express our emotions. In America, we spend millions of dollars on prescriptions to bring our feelings up and then bring them down. Have we lost our natural ability to cry?

I've visited countries where women drape themselves over reproductions of Christ, weep and wail while tourists stand back wondering what it means to weep over the body of Christ.

In some countries, professional mourners are hired to attend funerals to insure enough tears are shed.

In less demonstrative cultures, people hide their tears in the safe anonymity of dark movie theatres or cry in the shower so no one can see the tears roll down their face. If caught, they lie—"Must have gotten something in my eye," and turn away.

Go ahead, cry. Cry because you're sad. Cry because you're moving out of a house you love. Cry because your favorite shoes wore out. Cry because you're happy you got the job.

And, if you have held back tears for a long time, cry yourself a river.

LIFE AFTER FIFTY: A SECOND CHANCE

IT'S EASY TO CHIRP, it's a marvelous Monday, a terrific Tuesday and a wonderful Wednesday, but are you excited to turn fifty? The Big Five-O, the second half of life? Is it overrated or more important than you imagine?

As a youth, I remember hearing adults say, "It's downhill after fifty." Others argued, "Life begins at fifty!" These obvious contradictions piqued my curiosity. What's the magic of turning fifty? I knew the magic of turning twenty-one, but fifty?

One sounds like a warning: Live a good life before fifty, because after that, things become dismal. If I believed the other, life gets better after fifty. I preferred the latter.

Consider the impact of these sayings. Are you approaching the second half of life with trepidation? Or, excited to see what the future holds?

Once we've reached the fiftieth milepost, we notice changes in others and ourselves. Sometimes physical and sometimes mental. Vision might diminish. Backs might ache more often and digestion becomes more sensitive. Waistlines expand while hairlines recede. When memory slips, we find comfort with others who share similar experiences.

Turning fifty is life tapping us on the shoulder, "Wake-up. Hello. Pay attention. Life won't last forever." Will you wait another decade before you heed the warning? A diagnosis of a serious illness, or the death of a friend may be the wake-up call. Many ignore their mortality.

What does aging mean to you? How do you manage uncertainty and life changes? Have you signed-up for sit-ups and weight lifting, along with a morning walk? Do fresh veggies and fruits keep your heart ticking longer as the years tick away? Are you lured by cosmetic surgery and promises of moisture creams?

Couples married for many years often wonder, "Who is this person I married?" Men question their virility and women wonder what happened to their sex appeal. Becoming grandparents adds to identity issues. How did we get here so fast? Age can trigger emotional resistance and doubt. An antidote is to honor aging, cultivate a sense of humor to ease inevitable transitions. You are not alone.

If your marriage or live-together relationship is floundering after years of being together, admit it needs tuning. Re-examine your needs. Be honest. Share the highs and lows of your journey. Share new hopes and dreams. Relationships can deepen and become refocused and revitalized. Explore mutual interests and pursue individual interests. Married and miserable is a fast formula for going downhill.

Let's say you let go of a successful career and ask, "Who am I without my job?" This is a major hurdle. Without your career persona, redefinition requires attention and patience. Your job and career were a source of stimulation, an affirmation for fulfilling needs, a part of something other than raising your family.

Friend Lucille organized a group of friends to talk about how to rekindle our enthusiasm for life. She asked her friends, "What talents do you have that you aren't using? What are others doing that sound interesting to you? As they went around the circle they were pleasantly surprised to find themselves stiulated and inspired.

"I would love to be a mentor or a tutor for middle-school girls," one woman said. Another said, "I have business skills that might benefit a non-profit board?"

"I've been a knitter and quilter for years. Maybe I could start a small business, teaching others how to knit and quilt," another woman said, beaming ear to ear.

Once the brainstorming began, ideas flowed. Joining an organization or local group—master gardeners, bird watchers, hiking expeditions, cards and game groups were ideas that included partners and spouses.

Are you a budding city council member or interested in running for office as a county commissioner? How about volunteering as a traffic safety guard at the school or become a library assistant or reading tutor.

Some of us enjoy careers that keep us inspired for a lifetime. Others wake up after twenty, thirty or fifty years of working with little satisfaction and admit, "I wasted my best years."

It's never too late to enjoy life—to become inspired. From couch potatoes to recliner-lovers, you can give up channel surfing and explore new options. It's never too late to find a hobby or interest that inspires you.

Taking the first step is sometimes the biggest step of all. Don't use age as an excuse. There are ninety-year-olds swimming, walking and dancing.

Go back to school. Young people love having the wisdom of "elders" in classroom discussions. Young and old, we bring experience that boosts energy, enthusiasm and enlivens conversations. Even if the classroom teacher is young enough to be your grandchild, remember, we are teachers for each other.

Don't let ageism stop you. Pity yourself and you will find yourself surrounded by people who support your pity-parties. Like-minded people attract like-minded people. Supportive people attract others who support.

Even if you have a history of poor choices, new positive choices are possible. Make this your first choice: Be kind to yourself. Forgive yourself for mistakes and past foibles.

Life after fifty offers new opportunities. Sometimes it's as simple as improvement of existing skills. Do you love playing bridge, table-tennis, fishing? Participate and improvement follows. Become an artist. Grandma Moses waited until her 70s to express her creativity through painting.

Self-publishing is a wide open field. No excuse should keep you from writing that mystery and birthing a book. Write short stories, a novel or a memoir. Several friends of mine have published collections of family stories and they didn't write until their mid-80s and mid-90s. These books are keepsakes for family and friends. And, who knows, you might find yourself with a best-seller! Never say "never."

Now for the big question: Are you prepared to die? Is your "house" in order? Have you prepared a will, healthcare instructions and documents to guide your family through wrapping up a lifetime of legal details and relevant possessions? You want to convince yourself, "I've got another twenty or thirty years left." Yes, you might, and you might not.

One of the greatest gifts you can give your surviving family members is to put things in order. As a Hospice volunteer, I saw spouses flounder with no clue of the family finances. They didn't know where documents were filed, the names of banks, insurance companies and investment firms. "We never imagined him dying so young."

Admit your mortality and become a willing participant in one of life's most significant processes. Face the inevitability of death. Manage your affairs BEFORE death knocks. Write your obituary. Your family members will appreciate knowing an obit is prepared.

Yes, they can add to it, but give them information. They will be grieving.

Some people leave instructions for their life celebration. One of my friends left a list of music, readings, and even the bakery where a cake could be ordered. Make your wishes known, and it makes it easier on your family. Downhill may be where we are headed, but how we make the journey is ours.

Here is the most important choice: Be happy.

Abe Lincoln said, "Most of us are just about as happy as we make up our minds to be." Henry David Thoreau observed, "Happiness is like a butterfly: the more you chase it, the more it will elude you, but if you turn your attention to other things, it will come and sit softly on your shoulder."

Whatever age, life holds mysteries. The ever-changing process from birth to death is a grand sweep. How about celebrating the wonder of it all, each and every day.

MAD SCIENTISTS IN A MAD, MAD WORLD

From whacky to eccentric, we're all scientists. Whether you're one who stares through telescopes and wonders about the stars, or one who wants to understand the wiggly things under a microscope, you're a scientist.

If you're mixing a recipe and your laboratory is your kitchen, or you're experimenting with fireworks that evolved into the atomic and nuclear bomb, each one of us is curious in one way or another.

I base our "madness" for science on curiosity and questions. How does it work? Where does it come from? What happens if we do this instead of that? Endless questions stretch our limits as we reach beyond boundaries of the known into the unknown. Just when we think we've figured it out, we find much more than we ever imagined.

It's a mad, mad world. Take salt, for example. Essential to animal life, yet too much is toxic. We sweat and it oozes out from under our skin. Mine it and savor it. Cook with it. The Romans used it as compensation to their soldiers. We like the taste, yet it raises our blood pressure—effects our organs and how they function.

Science has invested millions of dollars and millions of lives in research to improve our health. Eat this, don't eat that. Do this, don't do that. Research booms into a diet industry that experiments by tipping the scale up and down based on liquids, pills, exercise, hypnosis, relaxation—you name it. Every diet is an experiment and we, the guinea pigs. So many diets end up wild and whacky experiments. Just when you shout "Eureka!", other mad scientists declare, "Don't do it; don't eat it; not enough evidence." And the research continues.

Pharmacology has researched and produced a wonder pill for everything. Instant happiness and peace of mind. Improved sex lives. Revitalized hair and skin. Life without pain. Eternal youth. You, the consumer, are a part of the great scientific pharmaceutical experiment. We are a part of this mad, mad world.

Remember the days when we thought the world was flat? Someone said, "Let's take a boat and check it out." Those early sailors were mad scientists, curious and willing to sacrifice their lives, drop off the edge, and prove the world was flat. There were other mad scientists on those ships, too, willing to go to the edge, but their hypothesis was that the earth was round. We know how that great experiment turned out.

Sometimes our need-to-prove-ourselves-right goes as far as the dinner table. Someone says, "Did you know eating chocolate helps you live longer?"

"No way," says older sibling, and we're off and running to find the evidence to prove or disprove the statement. Your scientific inclinations escalate.

Years ago, without an ounce of evidence, I argued with my older brother that he got wetter walking in the rain from the house to the car than I did by running. I'm an intuitive mad scientist. I get my proof from an interior gut level voice.

My brother argued adamantly, saying I didn't have an ounce of evidence to back up my hypothesis. Years later—maybe thirty years to be exact—he tired of my intuitive madness, sat at a table and did mathematical formulas and calculations to prove he was right. "Imagine that," he said, "You're right. Not by much, but you're right." Mad scientists even show up in family disputes, and eat their words. We're funny creatures.

I appreciate the case of mad midnight scientists like a fellow who wants to know why his neighbor uses loud tools in the wee hours of the morning. His curiosity wants to figure it out.

Who in their right mind is up at 3:00 am, grinding and screeching power tools, metal against metal? Did the neighbor's wife kick him out of bed, or did he buy a power tool yesterday and just couldn't wait to use it? Does the neighbor have a vendetta against another neighbor? Or, is he on a mission to drive the entire neighborhood nuts?

With our need to find out why, the scientific mind creates one hypothesis after another. Searching for evidence can drive us nuts. How many mad scientists do you know?

Consider the evolved, mad scientists. Those doing scientific research sitting on meditation cushions watch their blood pressure drop, their heart rate slow and their world fill with blissful thoughts. These enlightened, yet mad scientists say, "Try it." And we do. You and I, part of the great experiment —humming, chanting, om-ing along merrily, wondering if life is but a dream. Proof is in the evidence. The great experiment on the cushion only holds up if your bliss is sustainable when you get behind a driver that refuses to drive the speed limit.

We ponder and research existence, from terra firma to stardust to the outer reaches of the cosmos. We research the logic of life after death and speculate on lifetimes before birth. Some swear by logic and others by intuition. It's a mad, mad world.

We're curious. We want to figure it out, do it right, feel better and enjoy life. Like the curious cat, we know how to kill others and ourselves in the process of discovery, but are we willing to be responsible for our sanity?

It comes down to proving our experience is real. If you push the envelope, the envelope moves. If you think you can fly, you create a flying machine. If you hear music in your head, you sing, dance, compose music, create musical instruments or meet with a doctor. We live this stuff and love proving it's real.

If you think you're sick, you're sick. And the moment you forget that you're sick, something changes, doesn't it? Have you first-hand experience with feeling sick and a friend you haven't seen in years surprises you—drops by unexpectedly. Voila! Your attention shifts from being sick to being wildly happy to see this old friend. You are energized. You have forgotten being sick. The mind instantly changes our condition.

We're an interesting lot. Each of us a cast of characters containing unique DNA—the blueprint—the instructions for constructing every part of our bodies. We are exquisitely designed, as is every life form.

Who among us has tried to prove their God is the God? So many names including Allah, Jehovah, Yahweh, Lord, King of Kings, The Light, Abba, Shangdi, Omniscient, Bhagwan, Parameshvara, Vishnu, Satnam, and Divine Presence. So many emotional, political and economical struggles to prove there is one God.

Religious scientists among us say there is evidence that prayer works. It changes people's attitudes and their well being. Heals the sick and lifts those who are down and out.

It's a mad, mad world for political scientists who want to prove themselves right. We argue the issue of global warming, how to manage the environment and is legalizing marijuana a wise decision. Some want to revolutionize healthcare, abolish taxes and abortion. And, everyone has scientific evidence proving themselves "right".

I find it interesting that Earth is the only planet not named after a god. I also find it interesting knowing Dog is God spelled backwards—a cosmic clue to our evolution. Sit and stay are outdated commands based on space and time.

We are dissolving into a continuum where community and cooperation demand our awareness transpose the suppositions into new compositions. Dog is God. God is Dog. I am you. You are me.

Holograms and 3-D images are evidence that the two-dimensional world of right and wrong, you and me, them and us are outdated models. An evolutionary awareness is emerging. Dog eat Dog strategies are outdated as Sane Scientists take their place. The new model? God Is God. And DNA, our genetic make up, translates into Discerning Noble Action.

UNDER THE BRIDGE

ONCE UPON A TIME the Billy Goats Gruff made their way across the bridge, but not without dealing with a great, ugly Troll who lived beneath the bridge. This Norwegian folk tale gave us shivers as children. Now we're grown up. What do we fear or imagine about the Troll who lives under the bridge?

Who are the current day occupants living in the shadows of bridges and freeways, dark doorways and alleys, abandoned cars and cardboard boxes? They are the homeless—many whom we hesitate to recognize as our nieces and nephews, our aunts and uncles, fathers and mothers, veterans of many wars, and yes, our children too.

Are you willing to look or do you turn away? Facing the Troll may help you face the shadows of your life? Who are the courageous among us willing to venture under the bridge?

If you think you don't know these people, consider the notion of six degrees of separation based on the work of social psychologist Stanley Milgram in the 1960s. He set out to show that everyone on the planet connects by just a handful of intermediaries—which means, you are near to knowing the Trolls under the bridge, curled up in cardboard boxes, wrapped up in tattered blankets.

While workers at shelters and food kitchens admit knowing the homeless, most of us avoid eye contact. We turn away, unwilling to see, fear that homelessness might be contagious.

Homelessness is an uncomfortable topic. Most of us prefer to stay comfy and warm. A chill runs up our spines when we open the door to homelessness. It requires us to face the unknown, the core of our own vulnerability—our ineptness at dealing with a social truth.

Reported by the Veterans Administration, 196,000 veterans of many ages were homeless on any night in 2006. The National Alliance to End Homelessness estimates 495,400 veterans were homeless during the year.

Do you recognize these men and women? Have they sat at your dinner table, played cards with you, slept under your roof before the safety net—we all want to trust will catch us—fell out from under their feet?

Many of the homeless suffer from mental illness. Veterans who have seen combat deal with post-traumatic stress. Women and children deal with the trauma of domestic abuse—sexual, physical and mental. Escaping from their abuser, they are without a home. Sometimes they become entangled with drugs and alcohol as a way out of their pain, a way to numb their homeless realities. Are drugs and alcohol the cause or the consequence of homelessness?

We describe the homeless with judgmental words—skid row, the Bowery, hobos, panhandlers, transients, tramps and vagrants. It is a population crossing boundaries of age, race, ethnicity and gender—young and old, educated and uneducated, married and single people to whom life has thrown a curveball.

Once the homeless loitered or gathered in churches, libraries and other public areas. Their increased population has resulted in closed doors. Public toilets now limit hours as gas station attendants and shopkeepers keep them off-limits, accessible only with a key provided by a designated person.

Tent City 3, created in Seattle in 2002 by nonprofits SHARE/WHEEL, was the first legal homeless encampment, self-managed by nearly 100 people. The camp rotated around the Metro Seattle Core, restricted to private property like Seattle University. Tent City 4, created in 2004, tried to use public land but was unsuccessful in negotiating city-owned land. Now it moves every three to four months to various church properties.

Aiding the homeless in Portland, the city designated an encampment on city property near the airport, known as Dignity Village—a village of tents and built-to-code shanty homes for roughly 60 residents. In an interview with The Olympian, one resident said, "The more time you have to spend surviving is time we can't spend succeeding." This woman's husband was arrested and sent to jail for a hunting violation. She became homeless.

There are temporary shelters in many cities, even in small communities where crucial stopgap measures exist. Food and beds are provided for a night or more. There are women's shelters, shelters for teens, shelters for families, shelters for men.

Put names to faces. Look into the eyes of any of 800,000 homeless people in any given day. Are any related to you, or someone you know? Would one person be you or me?

If we relate, and make homelessness personal, might we see something other than the Troll who lives under the bridge? Might we see a family in need? Someone we could help while they get back on their feet?

Does poverty of spirit prevent us from going under the bridge, facing the shadow of life? Might we reconnect with those aspects of ourselves we disown, loath and avoid? And maybe there is something more important to this.

Are we willing to join, to bridge with the disenfranchised? Connect each to the other? Would Billy Goats Gruff become Lambs of Love?

It's time we create a whole new story.

Note: Although this was written in 2007, the topic remains a current concern we face.

■
REMOVE THE CLUTTER

ANY TIME OF YEAR is a good time. Spring, a terrific time to lighten up and let go. Time to create a path and remove the clutter. Get rid of the crapola.

For those with impeccable drawers, closets, garages and storage units, you get a gold star. Your clutter is "organized." Or at least, not half as cluttered as your neighbors, right?

Discussing stuff—the stuff stacked up or stuffed out of sight—makes most of us uneasy.

You may hear intelligent adults laugh, saying, "You think you're buried in stuff? I can barely get into my garage, the path is so narrow."

Another response, "You haven't seen too much stuff! My barn is stacked twenty feet high with things we haven't used in twenty years, and now we rented a storage unit." This is true.

We stack and stash it away — fancy platters, the duck-hunting vest, and your mother's lace doilies. All packed away for the day you plan to use it. The day never comes.

Most of us have a trace of clutter somewhere. I confess to a cluttered desk. I justify it as a catalyst for my creative process. Chaos is the precursor of creation, yes? Then comes the tipping point. I put everything away and start over.

Stacks grow taller until they block my garden view—that's when the reference books, borrowed books and books we love are returned to their proper place of occupancy. And the process begins all over again.

The dining room table and kitchen counter become drop-off spots for bills, coupons, magazines, junk mail, unfolded laundry and fat-squares of quilting fabric. What was this table's original function? A place to enjoy a meal with family and friends?

Where does this stuff come from? The U.S. Mail delivers plenty. There are magazines you plan to read, even daily papers offer bargains and a calendar of Friday garage sales.

Many of you bring home arms and baskets full of things you bought for pennies, stack it up and never consider what convinced you to buy the stuff.

And the secondhand, consignment store junkies, you know who you are. You rummage through shops and seek bargains. So what if you have three cast iron frying pans! This one is in excellent condition for the price.

Trinkets, antiques, art supplies, building scraps—yes, you will find a use for everything. Build something, or sell it for a profit. It's too good to throw away. Excuses justify the hunt.

From garage sales and secondhand stores, to the Cultural Clutter Collection Churches like eBay, home shopping networks, and outlet malls, we play lets-make-a-deal 24/7. No end in sight. Cupboards are stuffed to the max.

Are you a high-tech pack rat who sniffs out online music, television programs, movies and comic books? You pride yourself with ion gigabytes of data, downloaded e-books, e-pamphlets and e-magazines. Digital data gets stashed on hard drives, back-up drives, CDs, DVDs, MP3s, and memory sticks. The digital piles get deeper.

Don't bother confessing you save yogurt containers, rubber bands and cardboard boxes because you plan to use them. Good grief! Get rid of them.

If my words seem weighty, I hope they inspire you to create a path in your life. One drawer at a time. One closet. Make three piles: Keep, Toss or Donate. This saves time. Then work your way to the garage.

If you need help, invite a few friends. And, if you can't cope, phone a professional organizer. Start your own support group, take a class on how to organize your life, or visit a therapist. Last resort? Rent a dumpster and fill it up. Or, move.

May your path be cleared and your clutter be gone.

■
DO WE EVER GRADUATE

ARE YOU A LIFELONG LEARNER? Every September, a special excitement begins. A cellular memory flows through your blood. A mysterious calling says, "Time to learn something new."

I remember feeling excited when back-to-school meant a pencil case filled with No. 2 pencils and a three-ring binder filled with blue-lined writing paper. Students still use paper and pencils, and they use laptops, eBooks, and other electronic devices.

The tools change as do the teachers. We're in the School of Life every day with countless opportunities for learning. Let's pay attention.

We live, learn, study, and analyze. We practice and experiment. We flounder, cheat, flunk and excel. As poet Robert Frost wrote, "We dance around in a ring and suppose, but the Secret sits in the middle and knows." Do we ever graduate? Frost offers us a philosophical reminder to honor the mystery.

The hallowed halls of the School of Life offer doorways to endless lessons, big and small. You and I signed-up for this course. Showing up is optional. It takes willingness to stay awake and open your mind to opportunities for learning and growing.

Even the ABCs are challenging. We discover the alphabet forms endless acronyms. ABC might mean Art Before Chemistry or Apples Before Candy while to others it's a corporate conglomerate. How we interpret language varies. Consider the number of definitions for the same word: bat, spring, left, wave—hundreds of these words exist. And texting has altered the use of our alphabet—BTW, BZ, DIY (a whole new vocabulary). And, let's not forget emoji's.

As we age and wander the hallowed halls, we question, "Who's the teacher and who's the student?" It doesn't take much for a five-year-old grandchild to remind us to walk our talk. For example, you tell your grandson not to yell. A situation arises and you raise your voice in anger. "Grandpa, you said we shouldn't yell." Learning never ends.

We have the basic course called Marriage and Family, the one that offers many learning opportunities. We are challenged with lessons of love, respect, commitment and cooperation.

Marriage and Family, as a required course, changes with the times based on a population explosion. Selective Partnerships are choices we make, and children are optional.

Health Education remains a basic course. Most adults learn safe sex, personal hygiene, diet and exercise. Yet, many people in the School of Life struggle when they discover that Health Education varies from textbook to textbook.

Physical Education once meant push-ups, running laps—competitive and individual sports. Now it includes finger dexterity for text messages.

Driver's Education used to be straightforward: Learn the basics. Be polite. Use your signals. Parallel park and make legal turns. Now the course may include more lessons learned in courts of law, payments of fines and consequences for DUIs. And, if we can't control our tempers on the highways, we need a few lessons in anger management.

When too old to discern whether we're pushing the brake pedal or the gas pedal, it's time to retire the driver's license. Find other ways to meet mobility needs.

There are lessons we resist and lessons we find challenging. Math is one I resist. Practice is another. Math and Economics are joined. A paper checkbook is outdated. Debit cards, credit cards, Pay Pal and online banking have become the norm. Investment portfolios and banking are now managed with online accounts.

History is the past and there are those of us who practice a philosophy of Living in the Now.

Science and Religious Studies have merged. Our squabbling created a new curriculum called Spirituality. No waiting list for this course. You make it up on your own.

Pick any course. We've all got lessons to learn—patience, kindness, forgiveness, generosity, thoughtfulness and many more. If you need a tutor, there are plenty available. Remember, keep practicing. When do we graduate?

THE PHILOSOPHER'S GROCERY CART: FOOD FOR THOUGHT

IS ORDINARY LIFE A PHILOSOPHY LESSON? Philosophers love to quiry. Imagine a meaningful relationship with a grocery cart. First, you choose one. Oh no! It's this cart stuck to six others? Karma? Bad luck ?

Impatient, you jerk it with force. Then, you head for the produce department, grope the apples and grapefruits, pinch the avocados, squeeze the oranges, smell the peaches, flex the carrots, and tap the melons. How often do you take time to focus on your senses and enjoy the sensuous quality of life?

How many hands caress the same plum before someone decides, "Hey, you're the plum for me!" What influences your decisions? Do fruits and veggies shout, "Choose me," or, "I don't want to go home with you."

There are oodles of choices. Do you wonder why millions live with empty bellies?

On to the international food aisle. This is where world travelers shop alongside those who dream of foreign cuisine. It's the aisle where people read labels, trying to figure out what to do with couscous, falafel, masala, mole, and dim sum.

Oh dear. Here comes your next-door neighbor, the person you refuse to talk to—the town gossip. Or maybe it's that person you want to impress, and here you are, dressed in your less-than-spiffy best. Synchronicity!

"Avoid, at all costs," your mind chatters as you squat and act as if you are reaching for something on the bottom shelf, a doomed try to hide. As if a stealth shark moves in on its prey, you see the neighbor's cart advancing.

Your legs cramp. You rear up to relieve the pain, turn your back as this person approaches. Your hand reaches for a jar off the shelf. You bring it near your eyes, act as if you are far-sighted. You realize, "This scene is ridiculous. What am I doing?"

What causes you to descend into a child's game of hide and seek? Don't be too harsh on yourself. Most people smile and lie. They fake illness, groan while reporting, "I'm not feeling well. Don't get close. You don't want to catch this bug. Ta-ta." And off they go, skirting the interaction.

Do you consider what's going on when you avoid someone? Might there be a communication issue that needs tending?

On to the toilet paper aisle. How do you decide? Give it a good squeeze to find the softest product? Others spend exorbitant time comparing price per foot. In addition to softness and artificial fragrances, you consider one-ply, two-ply, extra soft, and texture. Bottom line, it's your bottom!

Here comes the cookie and cracker aisle. This is heaven or hell. You skip it. Your renewed confidence from having resisted temptation carries you past the ice cream and frozen dessert aisle. What a relief!

A brilliant idea flashes through your mind. There is evidence that high-fructose corn syrup is as addictive as nicotine and alcohol—why not add a use-tax? Will a tax on sugar-filled foods reduce consumption and improve health?

By the time you get to the meat, poultry and fish department, you count the number of carts weaving in and out. Each one seems to be moving closer to the meat of your choice. How can this be?

Another moment of illumination: This grocery cart is providing philosophical vignettes of choices we make as we navigate life.

Young shoppers hurry. Do we need speed limits in grocery isles? Others push and don't watch where they are going. Grocery carts become bumper cars when children do the pushing. There are the polite and the lazy who leave carts everywhere except in cart corrals.

You have spent 45 minutes pushing this cart up and down aisles. Mental fatigue is setting in as you join the queue.

You assess which lane has the least shoppers and dart behind a shopper who has two carts piled high. Clearly the next checker will be faster. You take a new position, hopeful you will save at least two minutes. The thought crosses your mind, "Why didn't I go to a self-check stand?"

Funny how two minutes becomes magnified. If we gave that much concern to time spent with family and friends, love and appreciation might flourish at home. Your foot taps. You whistle "somewhere over the rainbow."

It's your turn. Time to unload, stack it up and arrange the items. The black conveyor belt starts and stops. You wonder, "Who is in control?" Does it matter?

No sooner have you placed your last item on the belt than it stops. Smoked-scented woman next in line drops the rubber divider indicating, "Here's where my stuff begins."

Beep, beep, beep. Once again, the electronic scanner is working. Iffy belt moves forward. Brunette checker smiles, "Do you have one of our supersaver cards?"

"Supersaver" catches your attention. You punch your phone number into the keypad. You look at the register and expect a sizeable savings. The digital numbers show minus five cents.

You grin and consider the time used for supersaver cards. Is it worth the five-cent savings? And do you care that a computer somewhere registers your choices for who knows what purpose?

The clerk smiles. "Valued Shopper, you have saved five cents today." Does she want you to respond with, "Wow! That's awesome."

You return the cart to its corral. A woman's voice from behind says, "I'll take that cart from you."

As your hands release, an ordinary grocery cart becomes a philosopher's cart.

You stare as the middle-aged woman wheels it into the store. "Will she choose the plum I left behind?

TURNING OUCH INTO "YES, THANK YOU"

LIFE PRESENTS PLENTY OF OUCHES. But how often do you have to suffer?

Sometimes ouches happen when you don't get your way. Or, life doesn't treat you the way you want to be treated. Or, you want something different.

Suffering from an ouch is optional. Shakespeare was onto the secret of our freedom from suffering: "Nothing is good or bad but thinking makes it so."

How we think is the secret. If you misplace your keys self-induced suffering might sound like, "How could I be so negligent! Why does this happen when I'm in a hurry? Darn it! Where are those stupid keys?"

One self-recrimination follows another. You might as well cut a switch off a tree and beat yourself as to engage in this stream of self-abuse. Ouch!

To interrupt this suffering, become a finder. Find the source of your suffering and ask, "What was I thinking that sent me into this tailspin?"

Each of us interprets our own experience. What happened is less important than how we respond. Take the lost keys. What was your first response? Did you blame yourself? "How could I be so negligent!" Affixing blame does nothing to produce the keys.

Nipping these negative thoughts in the bud is the key to changing your experience from an ouch to something more positive.

For example, you realize you have misplaced the keys. Step #1: Stay calm. Step #2: Invoke the spirit of play. Instead of raking yourself over the coals, grin and turn the challenge into a treasure hunt: I wonder where I hid those keys? Are they in the drawer? Are they on my dresser? In my pocket?

I can't tell you how many unexpected surprises I've turned up while scouting for misplaced objects.

Take a moment to invoke the spirit of play or adventure and difficulties can become "yes, thank you." "Yes" because you are willing to respond creatively. And "thank you" because you are freeing yourself from suffering and learning to have more patience.

"Most people are about as happy as they make up their minds to be," said Abraham Lincoln. If we focus on the ouch, we live with pain. If we focus on what we can learn, we discover an ability to say, "Yes, thank you" to whatever life offers.

It's easy to become attached to getting what you want, when you want it. Yet clinging, searching, or longing focuses on what we don't have or what we're afraid of losing. These situations, by nature, create suffering. Attaching yourself to any idea or outcome limits your ability to be open to endless possibilities.

One of my favorite stories tells of a farmer who tilled his fields with the aid of a horse. One day the horse ran away. His neighbor came by and said, "It's unfortunate that your horse ran away. You must have bad luck."

The farmer said, "Maybe."

Next day the horse came back with half a dozen other wild horses. The neighbor said, "What tremendous luck."

The farmer said, "Maybe."

On the third day the farmer's son fell and broke his leg while trying to ride one of the wild horses. Again, the neighbor came and commented on his bad luck. Again the farmer said, "Maybe."

The next day the government came to recruit strong healthy farmers into the army. When they found the farmer's son with a broken leg, they left him alone. Again, the neighbor came and said, "Wasn't bad luck after all. Everything turned out well." The farmer said again, "Maybe."

By refusing to label these situations either good or bad, the farmer avoided suffering.

The next time there is an ouch in your life, ask yourself if you're willing to see it differently. Will you turn the ouch into 'Yes, thank you"—or, at least a "Maybe?"

TIME TO MAKE A DOGGONE RESOLUTION

DOGGONE IT! Another New Year's resolution.

Millions of people resolve, "This is the year I lose weight, exercise more, stop smoking, spend less, end family feuds and finish the half-finished projects."

Not me. Since I've worked like a dog for years, I'm resolving to live the incredible life of a dog.

Dogs are loyal companions, members of the family and best friends. The canine species has mastered the art of living in the now. Think of the freedom of being concerned with nothing more than here and now.

There is one exception to a dog's here-and-now lifestyle—the burying of bones and remembering longitude and latitude of the burial site. A great future investment!

I love great ideas. But, I wonder what I love enough to bury in the backyard for safekeeping. Where to bury it will be the biggest challenge, then will I remember where it is?

Speaking of memory, I am reminded of a small magnet that's stuck to my refrigerator door. It reads, "Never trust a dog to watch your food." I think it's me you can't trust to watch your food, so I'm giving up all resolutions related to food.

Dogs love to go for walks. Most prefer pausing at fire hydrants and bushes, leaving a messages. That includes every Terrier, Boxer, Collie, Poodle, Pit Bull and Mutt in the neighborhood. I will leave my messages alongside theirs.

Sniff to your heart's content is vital to the life experience of dogs. Canine critters stick their noses in your crotch. Don't worry. When I assume the life of a dog, I'll refrain from such behavior. I will keep my sniffing to the roses, pine needles and cedar boughs. True confession: My nose will perk up when passing the local bakery.

Applying dog commands to my life is an interesting proposition—especially sit and stay. When boredom sets in, which often signals it's time for a snack, sit and stay will be useful. Time to go outside for another walk.

Let's talk about treats and bones. Most dogs are selfish— not willing to share their treats and bones. I will, like a dog, assert myself with an occasional growl when someone tries to steal my treats. And, I'll give up the human habit of chewing the fat and take up chewing a bone instead. A sound weight loss program.

Dogs are loyal, dependable, and willing to express unconditional love—24/7. I'm willing to take lessons. Yes, I'll gaze into the eyes of those I love, but shaking my boodie as often as my dog wags his tail will necessitate practice.

Dogs love to be together. They are pack animals who romp and travel together. I value this quality. It's different from our American culture that promotes self-sufficiency and independence at all cost.

I appreciate how dogs work things out. Prancing, sniffing, dodging, crouching, ears perked up, hair on end—most of them don't take each other seriously. They adjust and carry on with life. Respect is encoded in their genes.

In dog years, I'm ten, so I'll command respect in the pack. I'm sticking with the idea you can't teach old dogs new tricks. Yes, I might roll over, but please, no agility courses. It's a dog-eat-dog world out there, and I'm already hounded enough. And, don't call me a hot dog, either.

What about barking? There are yappers, and then there is the neighbor's dog that barks and snarls every time he sees me. He's tethered to a tree. Would that instigate snarls? I'm sure I'd bark and snarl, too, if I was tied to a tree.

Give me my dog's life, any day. Yes, I'm willing to trust I'll be fed and doors will open for me. And I look forward to finding the best sunny spot in the house and basking there for hours.

Please don't apply the flea repellant. It wears off like New Year's resolutions.

LIVING WITH UNCERTAINTY

LIFE IS UNPREDICTABLE. Everything changes—the weather, our relationships, our income, even our bodies and emotions. Change is the one constant, yet we want to know what the future holds.

We want control over our lives, make choices, perhaps influence events and situations. Will we be safe and secure?

What's around the corner? Financial gains or losses? Lousy weather? We want a crystal ball to tell us what's coming.

With uncertainty in the world, it's easy to slip into anxiety. Attempts to peer into the future opens more uncertainty and magnifies our vulnerability, insecurity, and sense of powerlessness. Who wants to admit that we feel insecure and powerless. But we do. Admission of vulnerability is the first step to learning how to cope with uncertainty.

Next, realize the only thing you can control is yourself. Choose how to respond. Decide to be polite with a difficult neighbor. Economize by shopping less. Turn down the thermostat and conserve energy.

Major life transitions—divorce, job loss and death—often seem overwhelming. You think it's impossible to live with an uncertain future. The key is to experience your emotions, and pay attention to your thoughts.

Anxiety and fear are common when your familiar world seems to have turned topsy-turvy. Everything you counted on, everything you relied on has changed.

Your mind loves to spin a list of challenges. What you do and how you manage requires thoughtful consideration…
- Pause.
- Notice that focusing on the future creates anxiety.
- Stay in the present—here and now.

There are many things you can't change, but you can change yourself. When you notice yourself trying to figure out what will happen tomorrow, take a deep breath. Pay attention to simple things: I'm sitting in this chair. The clock is ticking. The cat is purring. Trees are swaying outside the window. Stacks of books line the shelf. My hands are warm. My breathing is calm.

Self-talk with focus on your senses helps bring awareness to the present moment. Tomorrow isn't here until tomorrow arrives. You are right here, right now.

It may sound simplistic, but this practice is powerful. It can free you from anxiety. Ask yourself, what can I do in this moment that relates to my future? If you worry about money, balance your checkbook or meet with your employer about a raise. Or, consider cleaning closets. Have a garage sale.

If getting a job has you worried, ask yourself, what can I do right now? Check the classified ads or call for an interview. Launder a shirt or copy your resume. Then, focus your attention on something unrelated.

Quiet your mind. Shift your attention to something else. Get out of your chair and take a brisk walk. Vacuum. Meditate. Phone a friend. Finish an unfinished project or play a game of solitaire. Turn on music and dance. There are endless possibilities within every moment—you <u>can</u> limit anxiety by refocusing your attention.

Uncertainty is an opportunity to embrace the present moment. Make a list of possibilities. Consider creative, cutting-edge ideas that excite you. Imagine something wonderful. Life as an adventure.

■
WILLFULNESS AND WILLINGNESS

I'M RIGHT AND YOU'RE WRONG. I want what I want, and I want it now. I'm not giving in—no matter what!

Sound familiar? Willfulness is bent on having its way.

Willful children test their parents. As a youngster, I loved orange soda. My parents didn't allow us to drink sugary, carbonated drinks unless we visited relatives.

Mother knew how much I loved orange soda, and given the opportunity, I might drink as much as three in a row. On one occasion, driving to my Aunt Marsha's house for Sunday dinner, mother said, "Do not ask for orange soda." Yes, she was imposing her will on me.

"We'll see about that," I thought to my six-year-old-self. I was a determined daughter developing a strong will of my own.

Upon arrival at Aunt Marsha's house, it didn't take long for boring adult talk to bring on my youthful restlessness. Legs swinging back and forth against the edge of the sofa, words spilled out of my mouth, "I sure like orange soda."

With an endearing smile, Aunt Marsha got up and headed to the kitchen, her words trailing behind, "Well, let me get you one, dear Ruthie." I can still see the look on my mother's face.

Will to will, mother and I clashed in silence. She glared. I grinned. My will won over hers. I did not "ask" for orange soda, but cleverly made a statement, "I sure <u>like</u> orange soda." Willful tactics are learned early in life.

Willfulness wears masks of self-interest, self-righteousness and the need to be right. They spring from a wish to control and have one's way with a belief of entitlement.

The problem with willfulness is that it's a response to a "no." No, I don't agree with you. No, I won't cooperate. And, no, I'm not happy with what you're doing. That includes the battle between mother and child, disputes between spouses, rifts between friends and firings in the workplace.

Even our health suffers from willfulness. We won't give in. We won't allow ourselves to examine our beliefs and consider new perspectives.

It's difficult to be vulnerable, to admit errors and prejudices. Instead we take a position and try to keep it at all costs. Sometimes that costs us a great deal. Emotions flare-up, angry words are spewed, blood pressure rises and broken hearts occur all because of willfulness.

Let me introduce willingness. The tingling sound of "ing" speaks to a softer, gentler way of being, don't you think? Try it out: Willingness to negotiate. Willingness to learn. Willingness to adapt and refrain.

End results? Relationships built on cooperation, open-mindedness, loving-kindness and togetherness. Think about it.

How often do you bump up against someone's willfulness only to find the same thing arising within you? Willfulness begets willfulness. It's ego. We huff and we puff, determined to blow down someone else's house just to show how strong our will can be. Bravado reduces us to acting like four-year-olds.

Notice your heels dug into the ground. That's a clue you're taking a willful position. Notice your stress level climbing. Ask yourself: On a scale of one to ten, one being not attached to your position and ten attached, where does your willfulness land on the scale? Willingness to change your position deflates that inflated ego.

Experiment. Let go. Ask yourself, what difference does it make? Keep your mouth shut and listen to what goes on inside your head when you move into a state of willingness. Feel the relief as your ego takes a backseat to awareness.

Remarkably, when we choose willingness, new worlds open to us. People become friendlier. Relationships improve. Your life has more joy and less stress.

Oh yes, Willingness has a cousin named Patience. Introduce them and you find time to slow down, be present, and explore alternatives. Invite feedback. Seek advice. Contemplate.

Willingness means you surrender a small part of yourself —the stuck, stubborn, heel-digging self. With a dash of patience, that growling, grumpy bear inside you can be tamed. Teddy bears are happier and more fun to have around. Be well. Be happy. Be willing.

■
CULTIVATE GRATITUDE

THEY DIAGNOSED LIN WITH CANCER in 1998. I was a volunteer with a community outreach center that offered free support services to people diagnosed with life-threatening illnesses. My role was to show up at Lin's home on Wednesdays at one o'clock. I was to offer a listening ear as she dealt with the cancer diagnosis and went through her treatments.

We sat on her burgundy, overstuffed sofa every Wednesday for nine months. She on one end of the sofa, me on the other—legs crossed as if we were meditating Buddhas. We faced each other week after week. It was not easy, but I listened as she journeyed through fear, hope, frustration, anger and so much more.

As volunteers trained not to give opinions, interject spiritual beliefs, or offer false hope, Lin presented challenge after challenge. She insisted that I share my beliefs. I felt shakened by her need to know if I believed in a God. She asked how I made meaning of life. Was I living the life I wanted?

We were both the same age, both single moms, both raised in southern Wisconsin—and then, here we were, brought together by this life circumstance in California.

I remember one Wednesday when she was particularly testy. "It's easy for you to show up every week and be happy. You're not the one with the diagnosis. You're not the one facing death."

I ached for her and for myself. What did we know regarding life and death? Her insistence pushed me to respond. "I believe we are all born with a diagnosis: We are all going to die. When or how is the unknown. I could drop dead leaving your house this afternoon. You could have a heart attack or choke to death—unrelated to cancer. I have no answers, but together we will take one day at a time. Maybe we will learn to appreciate every moment, every breath."

A palpable silence followed. Something shifted. From then on, we focused on the quality of each day, each hour we spent together.

Sometimes conversations turned to gratitude, gratitude for what we experienced in life up to that moment—the good, the challenging and the absurd. We shared stories of people who touched our hearts, people who challenged us and people who were pains in the you-know-what. We laughed, and we cried.

Together we were learning how to live. We shared stories of love, forgiveness and joy. We cultivated gratitude for our friendship, including our discussions grappling with cancer and death.

As the days became months, Lin softened. There were times of pain and struggle, but she focused her attention on gratitude. She appreciated simple details of color and textures in her home. She basked in the newly-found appreciation of inner silence. As she forgave herself for self-loathing and forgave the resentments she once had toward others, she softened. Her willingness to let go moved me deeply.

Lin taught me how to live and how to love life. She gave me the gift of appreciating the moment. Together we cultivated gratitude. Many times, we sat in silence and focused on our breathing, the simple rise and fall of our chests.

Lin died in the spring of 1999. Her journey to death had taken nine months—the time it takes for a full-term baby to be born. Life is an incredible journey.

As I write, it's spring—the season of birth and renewal. The perfect season to look and appreciate things that shows up in life.

Cultivate gratitude before death comes knocking.

———

The Japanese language has a word, on, that translates as a quality of gratitude together with a wish to give something back for what we have received. This experience begins with expanding awareness. Notice details in nature. Appreciate kindness. Pay attention to honesty, even if it's painful. See the light in your beloved's eyes. Notice laughter, friendliness, generosity, children at play, well-worn lines in the faces of our elders—everywhere, we can discover something to be grateful for, even the tough times.

Time to cultivate gratitude.

LIFE SOUP AND CRUSTY BREAD

GET OUT YOUR STOCKPOT. Prepare yourself for one of my favorite recipes. It's called Soupa, Soupa, Soupa. Not your ordinary soup, but something special that will warm your body, mind and soul.

It prepares you for unexpected guests. Not the human variety of guests, but the unexpected challenges that show up in life. You know what I'm talking about? Those things that show up on the doorstep when you least expect them. A telephone bill that slips into the bushes when you carry an armful of groceries into the house—the bill that is now overdue. The nagging, recognizable scratching sound you hear in your pantry at night—the little mice that want to share your home. Or, the puddle of water that won't stop pooling at the corner of the garden. How about, the phone call from the school saying that your kid is serving detention for the next three days for talking back to the teacher.

Yes, these and other unexpected "guests" will land on your doorstep—so, cook up this Soupa and keep it on the back burner, ready and prepared.

Begin with a large onion, finely chopped. The onion flavors the stock, reminding us that often it's the small things that make us cry. We might try to hold back the tears, but a good cry, even tears of joy bring powerful relief.

Onions teach us to keep a handkerchief in our pocket. There

is a time to reflect on what we're doing, time to wipe our eyes and time to blow our nose.

Next, add as much minced garlic as you like. Garlic is a mainstay to the Soupa. It's smelly and pungent, yet without pungency, life is boring and bland. Garlic, while raw and left whole, offers powerful medicinal properties, but minced and tossed into the stockpot, it enhances the richness of the soup.

Remember, we're talking fresh, minced garlic, not garlic powder or minced garlic from a jar. We want to learn the value of mincing—to chop things into smaller pieces can be a lesson in savoring the moment.

Instead of focusing on everything you need to do in the next year, mince life into weekly, daily and moment by moment pieces. Life is easier to manage—and tastier—bit by bit.

Next, a good handful of scrubbed and sliced carrots. Perky, bright-orange carrots teach us to be well rooted, yet reach for the sun. This balance is effortless for carrots and tricky business for you and me. We either get bogged down in earthly matters or lost in lofty, idealistic causes. The carrot reminds us to integrate what's above with what's below.

Now, chop three or four stalks of celery. Celery has tall, stately ribs and a green-tasseled top—a reminder to stand tall when facing the heat. Celery softens, though, teaching us that sometimes we need to relinquish our rigidness.

Potatoes. Pick out two big ones. They're filled with starch—the stuff that binds. Potatoes are of the earth. Their eyes teach us to look around and multiply our friendships. They teach us to stick together as family and community—essential for our well being.

Snip a small bunch of thyme from the garden. There's nothing like thyme to add flavor to life. I love it. Learn to use it with generosity, efficiency and wisdom. Put thyme into your Soupa and you'll definitely notice the difference.

Add 10 cups of water. Water makes up more than ninety percent of our bodies. By a modern miracle, we can open the tap in our kitchen and bring water from our rivers and mountain tops into our stockpots.

It's easy to take this everyday miracle for granted, but we cannot live without water and must learn to treasure everything it provides—including inspiration, playfulness, reverence and gratitude.

Oh yes, don't forget a pinch of salt—every grain counts. Season to taste.

There it is. You have every essential ingredient in the pot. This is your basic stock to keep on hand—on the back burner, at a moderate temperature.

Now, break crusty bread and enjoy the Soupa. It will sustain you, nurture you, and give you the strength and courage to greet your unexpected guests and the lessons they bring. Bon appetit.

PAUSE AND EFFECT...
TAKE YOUR TIME

ANOTHER MORNING MAD RUSH from a business meeting to your doctor's appointment. On to the gym, then meet a friend for a quick caffeine infusion.

Dash off to manage a pressing family challenge, your eye catches a ray of sunlight bouncing off the dew-covered grass. Unthinkingly, you pause and breathe in nature's beauty—fill yourself with a profound sense of well-being.

Pausing is both a natural response to life and a powerful tool. Within here and there is a time-out, an opening to surrender to an out-of-time experience.

Are you aware of the pause and its powerful effect?

I enjoy painting a mental picture of a janitor who's worked a long night shift. His feet are aching and he has one more hallway to sweep. He stops, props the broom against the wall, stretches out on the floor and puts his feet up at the same angle as the broom. For a few minutes, he pauses and rests. He basks in releasing the push of his work, honoring his aching body.

So many times during the day a pause presents what we need: a gap in time that propels us to appreciate being alive.

When I was growing up, my siblings and I wanted to get back outside and continue our play. "Can we hurry and eat?" The urge to dish food, eat fast, and resume life was our norm—behavior mother insisted we change.

Mother's personal style of pausing was saying grace before meals, providing the family with three spiritual pauses a day.

My legs jiggled under the table, yet there was something about closing my eyes and folding my hands in prayer that I liked. The ritual of bowing heads and waiting to see who would offer the prayer created silence—a silent pause.

What do such pauses mean to you?

Sometimes I listen to people carrying on conversations, with overlapping words and people interrupting each other. Then, everything stops. For a moment, no one speaks, and everyone feels the significance of the pause as a tiny shiver tingles up our spines. I recognize the familiar pause and its effect: People want to speak and be heard. The pause opens the space for that to occur.

When my daughter phoned, worried about money, my propensity to jump in and problem-solve was familiar. Learning to pause before responding afforded me the space and time to consider something new.

The silent pause creates a bridge between here and there—a place where we meet and every day concerns fall away. Often this space is where love, compassion and understanding arise.

On another level is the visual pause. Staring at the computer screen for hours—research, write, email, read the news—my eyes ache until something tells me to turn away and pause. Taking a moment to look elsewhere is a minor miracle that changes my perspective.

And remember the comma, the friendly bit of punctuation that slows the flow of words. It invites a pause, encourages us to consider the writer's thoughts before we respond. Ah, lovely comma, did you know you are the epitome of pause and effect?

We breathe in and we breathe out. Somewhere between the in breath and the out is a pause—and then we continue.

Right before delivering a punch line or getting the point across, a masterful speaker will pause. The audience sits on edge, hanging at the precipice. What comes next is captivating, spellbinding—an experience we long to return to time and time again. An effective pause cannot be ignored.

Could we use this spacious pause and stop our bickering and fighting? If we pause before taking a drink, a bite or a puff, will we be healthier people? If we pause between your words and mine, we build trust, respect and gratitude.

I'm considering using yellow traffic lights, the place between stop and go, as a visual reminder to pay attention—and pause. If you see someone lingering at the yellow light, it might be me, appreciating the pause and effect. And if you see a dog with me, trust it's all about the paws.

CONNOISSEUR OF FINE WHINES

IT'S EASY TO SNIFF OUT A FINE WHINE. Most of us recognize the telltale high-pitched tone. It betrays us, saying that something isn't going our way. Those within earshot often become uneasy and head for the nearest exit.

If our palettes could taste a fine whine, we might describe it as sour, bitter, and depending on how it's served and who is serving it, somewhat irritating.

Try sniffing out a fine whine in the grocery story. See little Paulie pulling at mommy's pant leg, "Mommeeee, Mommeeee, I want this cereeeeal."

Mommy becomes agitated. "Paulie-eeee, don't whinnnne!" she says in that high-pitched voice. Heads turn, and with military precision, carts swivel in the opposite direction. No one wants to listen to whining.

Who do you know that is a parking lot whiner? I'm willing to admit I can be a sore loser, too, when someone zips into my parking space, beating me by a hair. How dare she! That was MY parking space! My whine ages as I continue complaining for the rest of the afternoon—her audacity!

Pull up a chair at a bridge table and you'll find other varietals of fine whines. Winnie Whiner complains that lousy distribution caused her to lose five hands yesterday. Wilma Whiner complains to spouse Wally that he played the last hand poorly. And the marriage of fine whines lasts for days, weeks and years.

Ask any host or waitress what their special restaurant varietals are. Take Walter Whiner who wants tha-a-a-a-t table by tha-a-a-a-t window. He made his reservation a weeeek ago.

Mr. Whiner is in constant contact with the waiter throughout the meal. T-a-a-ke this soup back. It's not hot enough. The salmon is overcooked. I w-a-a-nt to speak to the chef.

By the time dessert arrives, Walter's companions want to crawl under the table to escape walking past the other long-suffering diners in the restaurant. Who is this Walter Whiner anyhow?

My guess, he's a political whiner—one who points a finger and blames everyone else for the country's problems. What distinguishes winners and whiners is winners act while whiners do nothing but complain. Common with politicians and political party patrons.

It's easy to forgive the whining country western singers because they tell the stories of everyone's broken hearts. Yes, we've been wronged, cheated, lied too, and abandoned. Whiners revisit those sad and painful losses, while country music keeps its hold on our collective psyche.

Don't worry if lost love is not your issue. The varieties of whiners are limitless. Corporate executives whine. They want their mega-million-dollar bonuses and golden parachutes. Forget they have lost other people's jobs and retirement funds. Forget they gave away the store, and have little conscience about driving the world's economy to its knees. They still dine as they whine, "We deserve those bonuses."

Then there's everyday whining that shows up at meetings. Notice the traits of whiners who love being asked for their opinions and the folks who get things done. Whining emphasizes the glass is half empty. Those with glasses half full don't need the whine.

Full-body whiners are a favorite. Sitting in their glass houses, they thrive on childish complaints. They boo-hoo when uninvited to this year's social gala, or complain, feeling miffed because their name wasn't mentioned in the social column of this week's newspaper. They grow huffy when they don't receive bows, kudos and curtseys for their contributions to whatever cause they embrace.

These connoisseurs of fine whine hone their complaining to a high gloss as they obsess over trivialities. I eliminate them from my garden party invitation list.

Big whine. Little whine. Subtle whine. From ugly hair days, to the coffee-isn't-hot-enough, to PMS pity parties, the whining continues. Terrible, dreadful days. The litany of complaints languishes in length and latitude.

Winners take responsibility for their actions. Whiners relish playing victim. Winners have what they want, and whiners want what they can't have. Winners find a way, and whiners find an excuse.

Life isn't perfect—but it's interesting. We all whine now and then. But try to remember, if you don't appreciate something, it's better to quit whining and change it—no matter how big the challenge.

Or maybe, look for the silver whining.

SHALL WE DANCE?

THINK TANGO, WEST COAST SWING, OR THE CAJUN 2-STEP. Maybe you're the belly dancing, line dancing, clogging or ballet type? Go for it! Get up and dance.

Sway your hips. Wiggle your belly. Dancing joins movement to music, from Brazilian rainforests to the Kalahari Desert to New York nightclubs to your kitchen floor.

People have forever danced, danced to honor the myths of gods and goddesses, lavishing us with costumes and transforming us with masks. We dance to change our moods, to invoke the sacred, to experience ourselves in the magical mixture of movement and release. As youngsters and oldsters, we learn to tell stories with our bodies, without words.

Whatever the beat, we move our feet. If hindered by self-consciousness, we finger tap and bounce our knees. The beat lives within our species. We are all dancers at heart.

What does it mean to dance your way through life?

Begin with these familiar lyrics: "Put your whole self in, put your whole self out, put your whole self in and shake yourself about. Do the Hokey Pokey and turn yourself around—that's what it's all about."

I can't think of a more simple philosophy for living life. The Hokey Pokey is a circle dance—no need for a partner, no stepping on anyone's toes. No wallflowers. Everyone can do the Hokey Pokey.

When you put your whole self into the dance, it means living life whole-heartedly. Do you give it all you've got or hold something back, "just in case." What holds you back? Fear of rejection? Failure? Criticism?

When you put our whole self in, you risk looking like a fool, yet brave enough to make a mistake. It also means taking the risk of being happy, radiating joy and living life to your fullest.

Learning a new dance is the same as learning anything new. Patience is essential. Practice! Go ahead, put your whole self in. The Hokey Pokey also says that you need to put your whole self out. Take steps forward, then appreciate stepping back. Retreat a bit now and then. Slow down. Let things be. Don't push to have everything your way. Learn to step aside, let someone else take the lead.

Putting your whole self out includes being willing to accept the ebb and flow of all things. Life has its ups and downs. The ins and outs are a part of accepting what is, when it is, instead of resisting.

The Hokey Pokey encourages a willingness to shake things off and turn around—good life lessons! Shake off doubt, fear and resentment. It's good for your health. Shake off old habits. Cultivate a skillful step that improaves the joy of dancing through life.

When you willfullly pursue relationships that don't work, or cling to outmoded aspirations, turn yourself around. This simple act gives you a different perspective.

When you're stuck in unhealthy relationships, stuck in poor employment situations, or stuck in beliefs you've outgrown, change direction. If you find yourself dancing to a different beat, be willing to laugh. And, if you've been dancing the same old dance for a long time, admit that it's time to turn yourself around.

The Hokey Pokey may not be what Baryshniko, Fred Astaire, or Michael Jackson danced, yet dancing through life is as simple and joyful as you make it. And, that's what it's all about.

KNOWING WHEN TO SAY NO

IT HAPPENED, BUT HOW? You said yes to the car dealer. Now you've got the keys, and you're mad because you got roped into saying yes when you wanted to say no. How did that happen?

"Yes" rolls off the tongue easier than "no", and sometimes "no" is what you need to say.

My father warned me, "Never loan money to a friend." And, there I was, listening to the sad story, watching tears well in my friend's eyes. How could I say no? I said yes, I will loan you the money.

Two months later, I knew I made an error. She packed up and moved to the east coast—no forwarding address. The eight hundred dollars I loaned was never returned.

When you say yes, do you mean it? Do you consider the outcome? Or, do you get emotionally drawn into the request?

Do you over-extend your time feeling obligated certain people? A boss, a relative, a friend? What keeps you sitting through a movie you don't want to see? Why do remain in unhealthy relationships? Simple: You say, yes.

Why say "yes" when "no" supports your integrity? Is it because your parents said no too often? Is it because you want to be the nice guy? Or do you want to avoid conflict?

Maybe it's about self-esteem—you don't believe you deserve to set boundaries. The kids beg to stay up past bedtime. You're overly tired, and instead of saying "no," you give in.

Giving in and saying "yes" plays out when we don't pay attention. Remember the person you met and your intuition said, don't get involved. Here you are, ten years later—married and complaining that you should have said "no."

Remember the time when a friend phoned and said she could get tickets for the big music production that was coming to town? Without thinking, you said "yes." An hour later, it occurred to you that you had another commitment on that day. Saying yes without pausing and thinking becomes a case of haste with a price tag attached.

Then, there was the time when someone you held in high-esteem invited you to a political gala. You said "yes," but got a queasy feeling in your stomach. The truth is, you said "yes" because you wanted to be with the power crowd.

Those queasy feelings eat away at personal integrity. It's time to learn how to say "no."

Your granddaughter is the apple of your eye and the peach in your pie. It's difficult to turn her down when she wants to buy the same jeans all of her friends are wearing. You would rather spend the money on a winter coat that she really needs.

It's time to use a "no" response. It's an opportunity to discuss choices, priorities and money management. Important life lessons can be taught when we say "no."

Imagine yourself becoming more skilled using no as an answer. If friends and family push your boundaries, thinking that you'll give in—the way you usually do—ask them, "Which part of no don't you understand, the 'n' or the 'o'"?

Learning to say no involves respect. Don't do things just to be liked or to be included or to look generous or wealthy.

It's okay to say "no" to people who keep urging you to have a drink or give them sex or loan them money or indulge in drugs.

"No" is a powerful response. Pay attention to your gut. If you start to feel nervous and uncomfortable, you probably want to say "no."

Notice if the first response out of your mouth begins with "ah-h-h." Hesitation is an indication that you need to slow down. Consider what is true for you.

A whole-hearted "yes" resounds with clarity, so notice the difference when your response is watered down "sure," or "okay." Check yourself to see if you are hedging to avoid saying "no." Half-hearted words indicate you want to say "no."

If saying "yes" is a habit, saying "no" takes practice. The next time you find yourself overwhelmed, your gut in a knot because you're doing things you don't want to, or you can't stand yourself because you're not following your own value system, try saying—"no, thank."

I think I'll take my advice. I won't say "yes" just because the experts say it's so. And, I won't say "yes" just because my family expects me to say "yes." Ah, "yes"—the answer is "no."

MENTAL FREQUENCIES

SAME AS RADIO WAVES, THOUGHTS ARE TRANSMITTED at different frequencies. You, the thinker, determine your own frequency, based on awareness and intentions.

These thoughts are picked up by a receiver—someone tuned in to the same frequency. If you are transmitting at 95.1 FM and people around you tune into 610 AM, you aren't on the same frequency.

Imagine that the people transmitting at 610 AM focus their thoughts on what's missing. They talk about what doesn't work and who's wrong and then defend their negative thoughts with excuses.

The folks transmitting at 95.1 FM have chosen a higher frequency, recognizing that fine-tuned, optimistic thoughts of cooperation and in-depth programming energize and inspire.

It's important to understand what this means. Everything in the universe is energy, science says—and that includes your thoughts. Thoughts drive your actions, emotions and general well being. Pay attention.

Consider two ordinary people. One wakes up saying, "Wow! I'm alive. What a beautiful morning."

The other says, "Damn, if today is as depressing as yesterday, I might as well stay in bed."

Notice the energetic difference in these thoughts. One is uplifting and enthusiastic, the other is energy-depleting.

As John Lennon said, "Reality leaves a lot to the imagination." And, Einstein pointed out, we can't solve any problem from the same consciousness that created it. The message: We need to raise our thoughts to a new level and learn to see the world anew.

How do we learn to elevate our mental frequency?

Begin by using your imagination and direct your mind toward thoughts that fill you with a sense of well being.

Who do you spend time with? That's a good indicator of your mental frequency.

If you're listening to lots of people complaining, explaining and excuses at lunchtime, consider the power of those thoughts. Dial to a higher frequency by lunching with different people and see if your experience improves.

Television, YouTube, Facebook, Tweeting, and Instagram are steady streams of mental frequencies that open you to invasion, thinking the unthinkable. Pay attention to the bombardment of negativity in some nightly news programs—words and images constantly repeated on every channel. How does this impact you?

Some time ago, a friend visited, and reminded me of the impact of the nightly news. She was surprised to find I don't subscribe to bundled cable packages.

The first night, she experienced withdrawals from the barrage of negative news she was used to watching. She didn't realize how hooked she was on "negative news." By the fourth evening, she felt relieved and calm—free of the assault made by some news programs. Less anxious and less fearful, she attributed the shift to less negativity.

She cancelled her cable service and reports that her general disposition and view of life is far more upbeat—happier. Would you give up the nightly news? Are you interested in an attitudinal adjustment?

Nip those negative thoughts in the bud. When gloom arises, let it go. If streams of negative thoughts eddy and whirl round and round in your mind, it's time to take action. Get up and do something physical—sweep the floor, dance, do push-ups or chop wood.

Physical and mental exercise strengthens your immunity against invading negativity. Include positive affirmations, positive thoughts. You can say, "When my mind whirls with negative thoughts, I focus on love and, "I accept myself unconditionally." Raise your arms into the air, stretching to reach a more positive attitude.

Take your mental frequency even higher by using thoughts to connect to something greater than thinking. Spiritual philosophies such Buddhism and Taoism persue the depth of thought by asking, who is the thinker?

Step out of the stream of thought and your thought frequency changes. You are no longer caught up in negative debris. Raising your mental frequency affords you to focus on your interconnectedness with life.

You are part of a global community. Now is the perfect time to direct your awareness to a higher mental frequency. Imagine a world without weapons, without wars, without hunger. Imagine sustainable farmland, healthcare, and education through cooperation, gentleness and respect.

Attitude dictates altitude—another way of saying your mental frequency determines your quality of life.

■
APPRECIATE THE SMALL THINGS

THANK YOU ARE KIND WORDS often left unspoken. Instead, we haul out lame excuses: "I'll do it tomorrow," or "Not that big a deal," or "He knows I care."

Nothing brightens a person's disposition quicker than a dollop of appreciation. It feels good to feel appreciated even if only a simple "thank you."

Appreciation has the power to magnify the small things and bring us together, heart to heart, even many years after the fact. It's never too late to say thank you.

I recall an English and typing teacher from my high school days. Hunched over from arthritis, he walked with a cane. That cane was more than support for his mobility.

He'd tap the cane against his desk, setting a rhythm for our typing speed. It was a humorous experiment, and he laughed as we struggled to keep up with him, or he with us.

One day, he banged the cane against his desk to get our attention. "Don't compare yourself to anyone else. You've each got your own tempo. Keep practicing, and you'll find that your skills improve."

Many times he'd remind us of this, and to this day, I appreciate him and the humor of his tempo-tapping cane. I also appreciate that he maintained a positive outlook and a wonderful sense of humor, even in the face of arthritic pain.

How often do you stop to appreciate the simple lessons you've learned and the people who have inspired you?

There is much to appreciate. Even the warmth of a blanket or the sound of a teapot telling you it's time to brew your tea are worthy of appreciation. Listen to the crunch of toast as you chew and appreciate your ability to hear and taste.

I find it inspiring when people shift their focus from what doesn't work to what is working. And…appreciate a new perspective. Instead of pointing out what remains to be done, express gratitude for things completed. Appreciation builds goodwill. It's the feel-good antidote to mending squabbles.

Why wait for death to come knocking when you can heal those long-standing family feuds by focusing on the small things you appreciate about each other? Don't put it off. Do it now.

When a friend shows up late because of a heavy traffic mishap on the highway, you feel frustrated and disappointed. Turn it around: "Hey, I understand how those things happen. I appreciate that you intended to arrive on time."

What a difference it makes to acknowledge a positive intention rather than turning your disappointment into shame and blame.

I'm sure most of us can find times in our lives when we've been on a valiant mission—riding our high horse, determined to prove we're right and everyone else is wrong.

It's easy to judge others when they're on that high horse, yet admitting we've been there, too, is a way to appreciate our human experience.

Appreciation is like one of those yellow highlighters used to draw your attention to something you consider important, to notice something special amid everything else.

Become a highlighter. Focus on the small things. Encourage the good in people. Comment on the beauty of our precious Earth.

Acknowledge the importance of giving to others as a way to express appreciation.

If you love your community, show your appreciation by giving back. Volunteer. Share your time and talents with the Boys and Girls Club, the Senior Center and the local Food Bank. There are many organizations that would appreciate your help. Gratitude generates positive outcomes.

Rather than overlooking that you appreciated a friend apologizing, or that a neighbor helped you, let them know how grateful you are.

And, don't forget to appreciate yourself. The person you see in the mirror every morning does a lot better with less criticism. Smile at yourself. Speak simple one-liners of appreciation as you look in the mirror. Speak enthusiastically to yourself, and it becomes easier to praise others.

I can't write about appreciation without expressing my gratitude to you for reading these words. Thank you.

TWO SIMPLE WORDS: THANK YOU

A CIRCLE OF GRATITUDE creates a family, a nation, and a world of appreciative and appreciated citizens.

How many times in a day do you say thank you, and how many times are you being kind or doing thoughtful things? Parents and teachers remind children to say thank you, yet developing a genuine heart of gratitude is an artful practice. Can you see through the "eyes" of gratitude.

It's a choice, a choice to value life and find meaning. Look with the intention to appreciate someone, something, or a situation, and express it through words and generous acts of kindness.

This practice is simple. It requires a willingness to focus and express. First, you focus on what you appreciate. What brings you joy and has meaning? Consider people who make you laugh and respect your need to cry. Review daily experiences you appreciate through touch, taste, smell, sight and sound.

Consider the pillow where you rest your head at night. Focus on the food that nurtures your body. Does your gratitude extend to the person who helped you change a tire? Or the one who gave you a hand when there was ice on the road? Or the friend who showed up when you needed a friend?

What is it that makes your heart sing? Your grandchild? Your dog at play? A sunrise? Listening to Rachmaninoff?

Cultivate a heart of gratitude. Focus on what brings meaning to your life. How often do you acknowledge your friends, your spiritual community, or your health? How often do you take the time to consider the importance of affection, appreciation, and acknowledgement?

Emphasize laughter and value tears as a means of showing your humanness and sensitivity. Be willing to laugh and cry whole-heartedly. Share life stories. Notice the sweet quirks of your partner. Be fully present and involved with life. All this, and so much more, deepens a heart of gratitude.

To live from your heart requires not only focus, but willingness to express gratitude. Sometimes a simple, silent response of gratitude—a touch of a hand, a pat on the shoulder, or a smile sends the message, "thank you." Practice saying thank you to the trees, the mountains and birds singing first thing in the morning.

A grateful heart needs to be verbal expressions too. Someone picks up the keys you dropped—say "thank you." Your teenage son hugs you, say "thank you." A friend tells you how lovely you look. Yes, say "thank you." The neighbor across the street listens as you vent frustration and someone takes the time to bring you soup when you're not well, be willing to say "thank you."

The practice of developing a grateful heart may include a day-end review. Review the abundance of simple, yet meaningful things you encountered during the day. Remember the friendly smile of the bank teller. Bless the ground upon which you walk. Give thanks for moments of silence and nature's beauty. Thank yourself for being willing to bring gratitude to the forefront.

If you want to learn from the great teachers of gratitude, observe the Guru Dogs and Cats. Dogs don't hesitate to wag their tail showing gratitude. And cats purr and rub against you. There are many ways of saying thank you.

The French say, "merci." The Germans, "danke." In Mexico, "gracias." In southeast Africa, "asante." And here in the USA, the most powerful words in our language are Thank You!

■
YOUR NEW LIFE, RETIRED

YOU WORKED HARD. Accomplished and saved what you could, and here you are—retired. Some of you moved out of the city, maybe out of state. A dream come true. Your new life. Congratulations!

In the process of settling in, it is often comforting to know you are not alone. Creating a new life is a process. Let's see how you are doing.

The first couple months of your new life feels idyllic. Plenty of time to unpack power tools, hang the family photographs, arrange the furniture, and buy a few things to make your new home feel like 'Home.' Your sleeping habits change.

No more need to head out at 5:00 am to beat the commute traffic. A new sense of relaxation has you feeling euphoric.

You begin to orient yourself—read the local papers, have coffee in various neighborhood cafes, and notice how friendly people are. Indulging yourself in day trips, you include a visit to local nurseries. Not only do you learn about native plants but you find out about the local Master Gardener's meeting.

Four- to six-months later, you realize this is not a vacation. Your friends do not show up for weekly golf games, daily walks, or Friday lunch dates. Your business pals aren't dropping in at the office because you no longer have an office. You miss the old connections. Melancholy creeps in, but you stay in-touch by phoning, texting, and emailing—encouraging friends and family to come visit.

The inevitable happens. Bill and Harriet email saying they will come visit in July. Cousin Ken and Phyllis ask to visit in August. Tom and his nephew want to try out their fishing gear in early September. Topping it off, the grandkids will come for Thanksgiving.

Everything is turning out just fine. You look forward to giving everyone a glowing report on how much you enjoy retired life. You successfully re-establish basics like a bank, auto mechanic, dentist, doctor, chiropractor, hair dresser, church, and a few new friends. You even found a local source for excellent organic food.

Between the fifth and twelfth month, a few disconcerting things happen. You wake with the profound realization you aren't going back. This is it. You gave up everything familiar—your security. A sense of sadness creeps in. Now and then, you think, "What have I done? Did I retire too early? What will I do with my life? Why am I uneasy? What is happening to my self-confidence?"

You try to comfort yourself, focusing on the many positive things you have found here, but these nagging thoughts and feelings of uncertainty keep percolating up.

* * *

Can you relate? Do you talk about these things or remain quiet? How are you dealing with sadness, doubt, and uncertainty? If you are concerned, know you are not alone. Most people do not take a course in Retirement 101.

Retiring and moving are two major life changes. To uproot yourself from everything known—a past of who-knows-how-many-years—is a major shift. Adjusting to a new environment is challenging. No wonder you feel unsettled.

Were you a business owner before retirement, with employees who counted on you? Maybe you were a teacher with a classroom full of students, or a successful auto mechanic, or a chiropractor with a long list of happy clients. Having been accountable and appreciated, enjoying a deep sense of satisfaction, and playing an important role in the lives of others will bring up identity issues when you abandon these roles. "Who am I if I no longer play this role? What does life mean if I'm not providing these services?"

Maybe you worked one job with one company for many years, and whether you loved it, or tolerated it, it was still your "security." It provided a rhythm and routine. Without this familiar association, you feel a deep void, a sense of loss. Grief is a natural response to major lifestyle changes.

If you held an important title in your pre-retirement life, you may ask, "Who am I without my title?" Yes, even a title becomes part of a person's identity. Feelings of doubt and insecurity may surface. This is common. You are not alone.

Loneliness, or a sense of disorientation, is a normal response to moving to another community, or out of state, or out of the country. Remember, you let go of everything that was familiar—including the people you met daily at the deli, the gas station, and the post office. Allow yourself to realize the importance of these relationships. They were an essential part of your life. Opening to new relationships takes time.

Admit to feeling challenged is the healthiest thing you can do. To deny these feelings may produce symptoms including anxiety, depression, panic, weight loss (or gain), nervousness, short-temper, and impatience. Spend time during the week to focus on new interests. Be patient and gentle with yourself. Give yourself time to adjust to your new life. This process is different for every person. Some adjust quickly, others take months, even several years to settle into a new lifestyle.

Making decisions is a process. Maybe you take a part-time job. Others assess their talents, energy, and interests and choose to volunteer. Those of you who dreamed of gardening might join Master Gardeners. Outdoor-types often explore photography, painting, birding, and hiking. Become a local politician, or an advocate, fundraiser or grant writer for agencies in the community. What is it that will make your heart sing?

Allow for a graceful transition. Admit to the challenges. Welcome, with curiosity, your new life.

HOW DO OUR GARDENS GROW?

A VISUAL FEAST, a palette of color and sensual fragrances are invitations to walk the garden path.

Flowers open to the sun's warmth. Dancing and swaying with the breeze—elegant, playful—reminding us that things bloom in their own time and there is a reason and a season.

The scent of a flower can open a floodgate of life memories—love, death, birthdays and more. Who can forget the waft of a gardenia, night blooming jasmine or the rose? So powerful, so distinctive are their scents that speaking their names can even evoke a memory.

Flowers attract our attention, including researchers who love to study their exposed, sexy parts—the orchid's Greek name 'orchis' means 'testicle.'

The essence of flowers lifts our spirits, brings joy to those who receive it. "Earth laughs in flowers," said Ralph Waldo Emerson.

Edna St. Vincent Millay's vow, "I will touch a hundred flowers and not pick one," requires more self-discipline than I maintain in the garden. From velvety roses to happy-faced pansies to graceful poppies, bringing a few into the house is a natural way to extend my ambles along the garden path.

As a child, I was drawn to flowers. An innocent four-year-old, I picked my first bouquet for mother—strawberry flowers! You can imagine her dismay as she explained that those flowers were an important part of creating strawberries. "If you pick them, we won't have strawberry shortcake this summer." From that day on, I let the strawberry flowers grow and picked the dandelions instead.

We make our choices with preferences based on color, shape, scent, height, and longevity of blossoms. Others fill their gardens with familiar varieties from childhood—no matter how well suited they are for the local climate. I wager a guess: flowers in most gardens are considered friends. We nurture them and weed out whatever crowds their space.

Whether we're aware of it or not, our gardens show our personalities. Each flower has mythological meaning.

Take the anemone. These little flowers bring luck and protect against evil. Mythology connects the anemone to magical fairies that sleep under their petals at the close of day. Do you believe in fairies? Your anemones hint you do.

The aster is an enchanted flower—a talisman of love and a symbol of patience. This star-like flower comes in a rainbow of white, red, pink, purple, lavender and blue with mostly yellow centers. Are you enchanted with love and blessed with patience?

Tall and stately, the gladiola's name is from the Latin word "gladius," meaning sword. It symbolizes strength and moral integrity. Do you stand alongside the gladiola in this regard? Or do you relate to its towering stems that evoke drama? Are you known to create drama? Do you know anyone who does? Do they have gladiolas in their garden?

Shakespeare's Romeo asked, "What's in a name? That which we call a rose by any other name would smell as sweet."

The cliché, *take time to smell the roses,* reminds us to pause and appreciate. The rose, symbol of love and passion, has long been associated with Aphrodite and Venus, goddesses of love. Who would not benefit from taking more time to appreciate love?

Roses have, for hundreds of years, conveyed messages without words. With slow-opening petals, they symbolize confidentiality and each color has its distinct meaning: red, the lover's rose; white, innocence; yellow, friendship and joy; pink, gratitude and appreciation; orange, enthusiasm and desire.

We whine and complain about weeds, yet our gardens are sanctuaries that afford us many lessons, including patience. Somewhere between the seasons, our gardens teach lessons relating to continuous renewal—in our own time. This is a gentle lesson to make the best use of the conditions we have to grow and bloom, in our own time.

As I leave you to tend your garden, take this thought from G.K. Chesterton: "If seeds in the black earth can turn into such beautiful roses, what might not the heart of man become in its long journey toward the stars?"

FLOSSING YOUR MIND

GOOD GRIEF! Just when you think you've heard it all, here comes mental flossing. We're used to flossing our teeth, but flossing our minds? Imagine getting into those tiny spaces in your mind, loosening up and clearing out the old, mindless stuff.

When Trivial Pursuit came out in 1982, half the world went nuts celebrating the trivia floating inside minds. In fact, we were so enchanted with showing off how much trivia we stored, the game creators spun off countless variations to keep us entertained.

Trivia focused on the silver screen and boomers, sports and Walt Disney, and themes like *Star Wars, Saturday Night Live* and *Lord of the Rings*. Questions spanned the decades from the 1920s to the 1990s. By 1988, 88 million games sold in 26 countries and in 17 languages including a Junior set, a Genius series, and another for Book Lover's and Know-It Alls.

The internet created global connections with the ability to explore, expand and learn beyond borders. What is this continuous need to "go beyond"? Is it a fascination with what's inside our heads? Or do we love to ask questions? Perhaps there's something deeper set in motion from our earliest days when we first asked, "whas dat, momma?"

Mental challenges and agility is an obsession for some, pride for others, and hope for keeping ourselves mentally active by doing daily crossword puzzles, playing Soduko, Scrabble and other math and word games—endless problem-solving.

Philosophers and psychologists say we question as part of our great pursuit of self: We long to know who we are.

Those who meditate spend hours noticing their minds and the endless thoughts flowing along like a river. We contemplate questions like, "What is the sound of one hand clapping?" Others ponder, "Who am I?" and still others ask, "Who is thinking this thought?" We listen for answers.

Most of us relate to the concept of "I." We realize we have a body and mind, and yes, our body walks and sees and registers feelings. The mind thinks and perceives. And most of us have considered there is an "I" pointing to something much deeper.

In mental flossing, we discover our spiritual beliefs. Often we find what we believe is no longer workable. We may have been raised Catholic, then explore other philosophies like Science of Mind and Buddhism. We discover ourselves as "spiritual beings"—a meaningful, life-altering process for many.

Mental flossing brings out beliefs dating back to our family-of-origin. We find outdated beliefs including "intelligent people are only those who go to college; children are to be seen and not heard; or marrying outside your faith, race or culture is taboo."

To venture out in the world, explore and gain life experience, many of the family-of-origin beliefs are uprooted and we change. We are pleased to find diversity enriches life. We learn there are many kinds of intelligence.

Mental flossing is a useful way to eliminate negative self-talk. Notice how often mind chatter includes negative messages like "I can't accomplish that," or "I'm so stupid," or "Nothing ever goes right for me." Diligent mental flossing flushes out these negative, self-defeating thoughts so we make choices affirming our well being rather than depleting our sense of self.

There are those who don't consider themselves political, yet mental flossing unearths staunch political beliefs. Politics is a part of our nature. It is how we organize ourselves—from our country to our community to our family. It involves values and how we treat each other.

Politics includes our relationship to other countries, resources, commerce, and the environment. Discovering our beliefs and asking questions in these regards creates a mental map showing us the many directions we take based on what we believe.

This process of mind flossing affords us to become alert and aware. We pinpoint where we've been and what direction we are going based on thoughts and beliefs. Flossing the mind can loosen old beliefs, flush out negative thoughts, and bring us peace of mind.

Note: I suggest you follow-up flossing the mind by feeding your brain. There are specific foods that benefit the brain like wild salmon, blueberries, avocados, nuts and seeds, and dark chocolate. But that's an essay for you to research and write!

CLEAR A PATH, REMOVE THE CLUTTER

TIME TO LIGHTEN UP and let go. Time to clear a path and remove the clutter. Get rid of the crapola.

For those with impeccable drawers, closets, garages and storage units, you get a gold star. Your clutter is "organized." Or at least, not half as bad as your neighbors, right?

Discussing stuff—the stuff that ends up stacked up or stuffed away out of sight—makes most of us feel uneasy.

You hear intelligent adults laugh it off, "You think you've got it bad? I can barely get into my garage."

Someone responds, "Let me show you my barn—stuffed twenty feet high, plus we recently rented a storage unit."

You stack things up or stash them away—the fancy platter, the duck-hunting vest, and your mother's lace doilies—all packed away for the day you will use it. The day never comes.

Most of us have a stash or clutter somewhere. I confess to a cluttered desk. I justify the piles as part of my creative process. Chaos is the precursor of creation, yes? This writing wouldn't exist if it weren't for my cluttered desk.

Stacks grow taller until they block my garden view—that's when the reference books, borrowed books and books I love get relocated. Then the process begins again.

It's easy to convert your dining room tables and kitchen counters into drop-offs for those bills, coupons, magazines, junk mail, unfolded laundry and fat-squares of quilting fabric. Do you mourn the table's original purpose—a place to sit with family and friends and enjoy a meal?

Where does this stuff come from? The U.S. Mail delivers plenty of recyclable flyers. Suggestion: Sort through that pile instead of searching Thursday night's paper looking for Friday morning's garage sale route.

Some of you are bartering aficionados ready to pounce on anything priced for pennies. Arms and baskets full, you bring it home, stack it up and wonder what convinced you to buy the stuff.

And the secondhand, consignment store junkies? You know who you are. You wander through the shops looking for a bargain. So what if you already have three cast iron frying pans? This one is a far better deal.

Trinkets, antiques, art supplies, building scraps—I'll use it. I'll build something. Or, sell it for a huge profit. I'm sure I can use this box of perfectly good bathroom tiles. This stuff is too good to throw away. Countless excuses justify the hunt.

From garage sales and secondhand stores, to the Cultural Clutter Collecting Churches like eBay, home shopping networks, and outlet malls, we play let's-make-a-deal 24/7. No end in sight, even when the closet doors can't be closed.

How do those yogurt containers and cardboard boxes end up in the pile? Good grief! Get thee to the recycle bin.

Technology encourages high-tech pack rats—those sniffing out goodies online—music, television programs, movies and comic books.

You collect gigabytes of data, downloading e-books, e-pamphlets and e-magazines. All that digital data gets stashed on CDs, DVDs, MP3s, iPods memory sticks back-up drives and iCloud. And you complain, "Why can't I find that photo I took in Yellowstone?"

If my words weigh you down, consider making space. One drawer at a time. One closet. Make three piles: Keep, Toss or Donate—speed up the process. Gradually work your way to the garage.

If you need help, invite a few friends. And, if the stash is beyond your ability to cope, phone a professional organizer, start your own support group, take a class on how to organize your life, or visit a therapist. Last resort? Rent a dumpster and fill it up. Or, move.

May your path be clear and your clutter be gone.

Oh yes, remember to clean the windows so you can see your way to the garden. Enjoy an uncluttered life!

THE GREATEST SHOW ON EARTH

IMAGINE COMING INTO LIFE and picking out a costume. Your father reached into the wardrobe and pulled out a three-piece suit. You donned a white lab coat with a stethoscope. And others chose artist smocks, ballet tutus, firefighter helmets, and chef aprons.

But did we imagine that in these costumes we'd be circus characters? That we signed up to play our part in life's Big Show, the Greatest Show on Earth.

We've been juggling and balancing events and situations with families and friends for as long as we can remember.

When we signed up for this Show, balancing between two galloping horses may not be what we imagined. Yet, there we are, reins of life in hand, prancing with enthusiasm. Suddenly, we realize how vulnerable we are. One foot here and the other there, trying to stay upright, move forward, and look good doing it. What a predicament.

Other times, we seem to be high above everyone else—all eyes looking at us—we stand on that platform expecting to take a leap. The tension mounts. Do we marry, or not? Vote yes or no? Take the job, or keep looking? Is it time to take a risk?

It's a great leap of faith to thrust ourselves into space—reach, stretch, grab the trapeze like we know what we're doing. Then, we soar through the air with the greatest of ease. Oops! Something weakens our hold. Everyone gasps, anticipating our fall, and we pray there'll be a net to catch us.

More often than not, we land on our feet. Yet, some of us need to join hands to break the fall—families, faith, and our friends to assist the landing.

From the tension of the high wire, the calliope below reminds us to take our turn, become a clown. Big red nose, floppy shoes and a necktie drags along the ground. We trip over ourselves—beep, squeak, honk and flail. Twisting and turning our gestures remind us to lighten up and have a good time.

That was Ring Number One. Now for Ring Number Two. With top hat and whip, we enter the cage with roaring tigers and lions. With a smile on our face, we crack the whip, raise our palm and command the roaring beasts to sit up on their haunches, take notice—obey me!

Applause erupts, we bow, and silently pray the wild beasts won't turn on us. Is this cavorting and posturing worth the risk?

Then we change costume and strap on the shoulder-suspended tray, climbing up and down the aisle steps shouting, "Peanuts! Popcorn! Cracker Jacks!"

Everyone wants to buy what we offer. The sale requires us to reach across four people, exchanging goodies for coins. We do the reaching and the passing. Some things taste better when there is a stretch in the give and the take.

A voice booms, "Ladies and gentlemen, now appearing in the main arena, the acrobats!" Agile and lithesome, flexible and faultless. We expect to come somersaulting and cartwheeling into the ring, as if the body will last forever. After all, this is the greatest show on earth.

A few somersaults later, it's time to carry not one, not two, not three but four people on our shoulders. The guy at the top is getting applause for juggling three burning torches. We're at the bottom of the pyramid carrying the rest and ignoring our aching backs.

Never mind the dust being kicked up by the elephants. We have people depending on us, who need our strength. The Show goes on.

And then it happens. Elephants setting themselves free. In the panic, the vendor throws up his tray. Peanuts everywhere. Elephants and audience smashing and mashing and squishing the hundreds (maybe thousands) of peanuts, turning them into liquid butter. Peanut butter! Where's the jelly? The Show must go on!

MENTAL PLUMBING

I HAVE AN IDEA TO WRITE A MANUAL—The Mental Plumbing Manual. It will include strategies for overcoming sleepless nights and preventing our minds from whirling and swirling.

It's time we learn how to take care of what I call our mental plumbing.

Outdated, repetitive thoughts are as annoying as drippy faucets or leaky toilets. Even worse than annoying are those wretched thoughts that create drippy pools of anxiety, worry and discontent.

My mental plumbing manual will include two disclaimers: Tongue-in-cheek. Use at your own risk.

This manual will not be a simple synthesis of esoteric books guaranteeing enlightenment. My mental plumbing manual will contain profound instructions: "Think long and hard" and "You'd better think twice," not to mention the deep wisdom of "Don't give it another thought."

Our minds are plumbed for thinking, thinking, thinking—but what are we thinking? Who spends hours thinking about what everyone else is thinking? Good grief, will someone please call the plumber to relieve this mental constipation?

Some want fast track mental relief. Call the doctor. Ask if mental contagions are going around. The more congested your thoughts, the quicker they turn into pathogens, creating disease within your body. Funky thinking deteriorates relationships with family and friends.

Like colds or the flu, thoughts move through the air. All it takes is one person entering the room thinking positive thoughts and, the next thing you know, everyone in the room feels uplifted and inspired. Whether they're positive or negative, thoughts are contagious.

Notice the changes that come with a person thinking negative thoughts? A foreboding heaviness creeps into the room like a dark cloud obscuring the sun. We get an eerie feeling that we are being infected by a murky contagious condition.

Both ancient mystics and modern day teachers repeat the same advice: "Change your thinking and change your life." I suggest the key to this change is first become familiar with your mental plumbing and how to keep it clean and flowing smoothly.

But where do we find the blueprints for this complex mental plumbing system and learn to move from blockage to being in the flow?

The few master plumbers I've known recommend that we install mental flow controls and filters.

One mental flow control involves learning how to sit in silence. Sit on a cushion on the floor, legs folded like elbow fittings, eyes closed, silently observe your thinking without becoming attached to any thought.

This flow control makes you aware of your thoughts. Notice the contagions and prevent them from getting stuck by letting them flow. Thinking becomes nothing more than thinking.

Another mental flow control is self-inquiry. When you replay the same old thoughts and become distracted by them, ask, "What am I thinking?" Identifying thought patterns brings awareness. Repetivie thoughts, like sewage, close the system.

There is a connection between thoughts and emotions. If you focus on the past, your mental plumbing backs up. Emotions overflow when they have nothing to do with current time.

Rooting out the past can help redirect your thinking to present time. This eases emotional suffering. Controlling your thoughts can be as simple as redirecting your attention to an activity—dance, chop wood, play the piano. Any simple but absorbing activity will relieve mental constipation.

If you find yourself stuck in a tank of self-righteous thoughts, observe how they multiply. They even divide people and communities. My manual will recommend that we purify these thoughts with large doses of humility. Not humidity—tears and fears.

If you are a slow learner, that's okay. Remember the optimistic book from childhood, *The Little Engine That Could?* This simple, moral story inspired us to believe we could climb every mountain. Just repeat, "I think I can, I think I can, I think I can."

Sometimes you need positive, repetitive thinking. It scours out the mental scum by removing negative thinking and encourages your ability to be in the flow. Scouring away that residue brings back your plumbing's natural shine.

If you find yourself blaming the negative thinkers for creating the mess you're in, you are adding to the mental constipation.

Leonardo da Vinci believed creative possibilities exist in the space that opens when you let go of your preconceived thoughts and opinions. Nurturing this practice, strengthens your mental plumbing and helps make it more flexible.

Getting into the flow while changing and adjusting your thinking might need some genius. This may be an important juncture where you need to invent new curves and connections in your mental plumbing. How about installing flexibility so the plumbing system is efficient?

One way to expand mental plumbing is to become friends with ambiguity. How well do you do when waiting to hear the results of a medical exam or the results of a college entrance test? Notice your thoughts when you consider downsizing the business or want changes in a significant relationship. What thoughts run through your mind? Do you become anxious? How do you respond to ambiguity?

By monitoring intolerance for ambiguity, pay attention to how many times during the day you use the words "always," "must," "never," and "absolutely." Notice if you end a conversation with a question or a statement. This practice brings awareness to how flexible your mental plumbing is.

Face paradox. For example, consider the saddest moments of your life and the most joyful moments. What is the relationship between the two? Can you feel the difference? Leonardo once wrote, "The highest happiness becomes the cause of unhappiness." Do you agree?

Stimulating mental plumbing produces great flow. Nothing becomes an obstacle. You become an open vessel. Instead of just listening to music, you might consider drawing shapes and colors evoked by the sound.

Play with transpositions. If your mother became a great artist who would she be? If your dog were a bird, what bird would he be?

Use thoughts to bring awareness to your body. Describe your posture, your heartbeat, and the position of your arms, legs, feet and hands. Interrupt the worn out patterns with sensory awareness. Take a few deep breaths. Close your eyes tight; then open them wide. Listen to the sounds you hear right here, right now. When your senses are active, your mind functions at a high level of awareness.

If you want to probe your mental plumbing, my manual will suggest that you create a list of provocative questions. For example: What is one thing I could stop doing, or do, that could improve the quality of my life? How can I best serve others? What legacy do I want to leave? What are the blessings in my life?

When you find yourself stuck in mental sludge, take out your list of questions and write out your answers. This process stimulates and inspires new ideas.

I confess, I am still an apprentice with mental plumbing. Whether I ever write the manual or not, I recommend that you eliminate the old mental debris. Yes, what you think is what we get.

■
GREAT TEACHERS AND LIFE LESSONS

WEDGED BETWEEN THE SCREEN DOOR and the front door, I shouted an offensive word at a neighbor boy. I was only four or five years old, angry-as-the-dickens about what, I don't remember.

In a flash, my mother picked me up, tucked me under her arm, and marched to the kitchen sink. Before I could say "boo," she had a bar of soup in my mouth. "Don't you ever say that word again," she said with a force I still remember today.

That was the day I learned that the taste of soap is something I never want in my mouth again. But, I can't say the soap cured me 100% over my lifetime of ever using a few disdainful words when angered. What I learned is that I wouldn't want to be within earshot of my mother if I ever used the word again.

Our lessons begin the day we're born and continue throughout life. Some more painful to learn than others.

When I was a college student in southern Wisconsin, a new friend from Attleboro, Mass. invited me to travel to visit her family over spring break.

Arriving in Boston, the plan was to rent a car and her parents planned to reimburse me at the end of our stay. I was the one "of age," so I signed the rental contract at the airport. Young, innocent and trusting, I didn't give it a second thought.

When the vacation ended, my friend's parents were to drop us at the airport and return the car. Since they agreed to pay for it, I assumed there would be no problem. Never, ever assume anything!

Three weeks later, I received a phone call from the rent-a-car agent, wondering where the car was.

"What?" I gasped in disbelief. I didn't have a clue where the car was, but you can imagine how fast I dialed my friend to find out what was going on.

Her parent's car needed repair, she said, and they kept the rental car until the repairs were made. Not to worry, she assured me. "They will return the car and pay for it."

The car wasn't returned for another fifteen days—thirty-five total rental days! And, the saga continued. When the time came, they couldn't pay the charges. The contract was in my name. I was responsible.

As a college student, I didn't have the money. My parents bailed me out, and I made payments to them for months afterwards.

My friend quit school and returned to Attleboro. It was a sad and disappointing experience. I learned a few painful lessons: Don't assume that adults—even the parents of friends—will act responsibly. Never sign a contract unless *you* have the money to pay. Don't assume that friends will help you out. Don't assume anything.

And you? What lessons have you learned in life? Who were your teachers? Most of us fall in love and suffer at least one broken heart. What lessons did you learn?

Some decide to never love again. Others become bitter and distrust the opposite sex. There are those who learn that a partner can't meet all your needs. It's important to have other friends to spend time with when your spouse or partner doesn't share your interest in fishing or walking or playing bridge.

And, there are those who learn to work with relationship challenges, nurture each other, and enjoy a meaningful, lifetime relationship. Who have been your teachers when it comes to love?

Have you learned a trade or craft? Who taught you your skills? Who taught you to appreciate art and beauty, to love music and respect nature? In high school, Mr. Meythaler taught typing. I loved it and was soon typing ninety-words a minute. When I needed a job during college, a printing company hired me as a typesetter. The owner said, "I'll teach you a trade and you will never be without work."

I didn't have a clue that the writing, graphic design, and publishing skills he taught would bring me great joy. We don't know when we are young that some lessons will serve us for a lifetime?

Same goes for parenting. What most of us know about parenting as new parents pales to what we learn from our kids over the course of a lifetime. Children are living lessons in spontaneity. Forget planning. They live every uncertain moment with a spirit of wonder while we adults struggle to maintain control and follow a schedule.

Children try new things and are forever testing the waters. They don't restrict themselves. Somewhere along the path of growing up, some of us hesitated, became fearful of taking risks. We convinced ourself that we can't jump in and participate unless we're "qualified." We think we need a degree or a certificate or a license to play. Interesting how we stop ourselves from exploring, imagining and experimenting.

Animals are great teachers. I've learned valuable lessons from my golden retriever, Rumi. He was a master teacher, giving me lessons on the value of taking walks, learning to sit and stay (is that called commitment?) and expressing appreciation. I've yet to master the tail wagging, but he taught me the nature of unconditional love.

Yes, cats are great teachers, too. The art of gazing out the window, purring when contented, taking frequent naps and doing yoga stretches are among the valued lessons from our feline friends. Oh yes, independence is a feline attribute many of us have yet to learn. We are often slow learners.

It's Mother Nature, though, who drives home lesson after lesson, humbling us with her power and presence. We build houses on cliff sides, river banks, deltas, and beaches. When the bluffs erode, the water rises and the hurricanes roar in, we're somehow surprised and stunned. Why do we keep repeating the class in rebuilding? Is Mother Nature trying to teach us something that we fail to learn?

Many people believe our finite planet has limitless resources. If one oil field, or one water well dries up, we have the notion we can keep on drilling. We move from here to there without connecting the dots of supply and demand. How many oil fields, water tables, wells and rivers need to dry up before we learn the lesson?

It's finally dawning on us that the Earth is not a straight line that leads to infinity. She is a living sphere, an organism, that some call Earth and others call Gaia. The living body beneath our feet pulsates, belches and overflows. She trembles, shakes and cracks. She sparkles, feeds and breathes.

Her soils and seas are mighty, yet fragile. We are facing serious, unprecedented lessons as toxic waste, toxic herbicides, and trash flotillas in the sea are choking off the source of food for us and other creatures.

If we keep abusing and exploiting this Being beneath our feet, bleeding her dry of natural resources, our inattention will have a staggering price. Yes, we may rebuild houses. But, as living organisms, if we don't learn the lessons Mother Nature tries to teach us, we will suffer the consequences.

On a smaller scale, I notice the wild blackberry branches that creep through fences from my neighbor's yard, winding their thorny tentacles into my greenhouse. Their lesson? Life can get prickly if we don't pay attention.

Maybe it's time we pay closer attention to the lessons of the Earth. We call her Mother, but often treat her with disrespect. We say we love her, but we use up everything we can lay our hands on and then trash and burn the rest as we go.

I know it's painful to look at our negligence. We want a good life, and if the Earth, our home planet and greatest teacher, is telling us to pay attention, are we willing to become learned students? If not now, when?

WHAT DO YOU CALL HOME

IF YOU WERE DOROTHY, and clicked your heels together, you might call Kansas your home. And if your name were E.T., you'd look at me with wide eyes and ask, "E.T., call home?"

What you call home depends on many things. Just because the waitress has a southern drawl doesn't mean she calls Louisiana home. When asked, "Where is home?" she answers, "I grew up in South Carolina, then moved to upstate New York, and five years later moved to Alaska. From there, I moved to California. Fifteen years later, I was in Oregon. And, for three months now, I call Port Townsend home."

I found her journey interesting. For some, like the turtle, "home" is wherever you are.

We've all heard, "Home is where the heart is." A friend said, "Gosh, I moved around all my life—I'm an Air Force brat. I don't have a place I call 'home'." Then he adds, "Guess it's where I hang my hat." As a newcomer, how long does it take to call this place home?

For most of us, the word home evokes an emotional response: melancholy to bitterness, sadness to longing, and comfort to peace. Mental pictures range from mom in the kitchen to dad sacked out on the couch. Or, both parents working—rarely are both home at the same time.

From backyard games to tussles in the living room on rainy days, home is how we relate. From tucking under your dad's arm to being pushed away by your brother, home is sometimes tender and sometimes painful. Most of us remember birthday parties and holidays—visits from aunts, uncles and cousins on special occasions. For many people, neighborhoods and communities are included in the definition of home.

Home is the stuff we grow up with—the foundation under our feet, so to speak. The familiar—the "stuff" we hold near and dear. Generational recipes, dining room table, an antique bed in the guest room. The family Bible and family photographs on the walls. What comes to mind when you think of "home?"

Home is long-established traditions and rituals. Spring cleaning, meal preparation, financial matters, birthdays, marriages, death and family communication.

A fork or chopsticks. Leaving shoes at the door. Or praying before meals are traditions integral to the sense of home.

Raised in a home where parents respect each other, chances are respect will be part of the home you create. If your parents nag and argue, you may associate that behavior with "home." What was familiar at home in your formative years is often replicated in your adult life.

You may decide to do things differently and marry a soft-spoken person, a good listener. A few years later, this spouse asks you to stop arguing—the thing you didn't want to do! Familial traits crop up. It's easy to revert to old behaviors from your family of origin. Experiment. Notice family behaviors. Will they become make-it or break-it factors in future relationships and lead to "broken homes?"

The strength of "home" involves values and how differences are managed. From buying a bungalow to a mansion, from living in downtown Portland to a farm in North Dakota, we have our preferences. From meal preparation at specific hours to a help-yourself-anytime attitude, "home" means everything from structure to chaos. Sharing chores runs a gamut between gender assignments to rotations of doing what appeals to you. Family traditions run deep. Religious practices, holidays, and hierarchy based on age influence family structure and the quality of home life.

Your idea of "home" may look different than others. It may evoke "warm and cozy." To some, it appears as chaos and conflict.

Technology has expanded our definition of "home" to the Earth. Will another planet one day be called "home"?

I find it interesting to consider the variations, ideas, and beliefs that make up "home."

For me, "home" conjures up muggy summer nights and the sound of crickets…playing games with kids in the neighborhood…building snow igloos…marching in the Memorial Day parade, and participating in Swiss heritage celebrations.

Dorothy, from the *Wizard of Oz* reminds us, "There is no place like home!"

STICKS, STONES AND WORDS

CHILDREN ON THE PLAYGROUND SHOUT, "Sticks and stones may break my bones but words will never hurt me."

It seems to me that's simply not true. It doesn't take many words these days to get adults rattled, upset and defensive. Because we live in times of such uncertainty, we all have our personal list of topics that seem to readily push us into reacting and saying things that cause hurt feelings.

Environmental issues, worries about the housing market, the economy, wars, homeland security, immigration, healthcare, social security—you name it, we deal with an onslaught of challenges. And how well do we communicate with each other?

Schools are dealing with a rise in aggressive behavior—bullying. Bullies are those who are quick to anger. Those who want to gain power over others by dominating them with verbal and emotional threats.

Are bullying children a reflection of adults who dominate and disrespect? Are playground bullies sending us a loud and clear message that aggressive behavior is harmful to the health of everyone? Mean-spirited words do hurt.

Special interest groups point fingers at one another, accusing the other of being responsible for creating problems, while the Red and Blue contingents throw verbal sticks and accusatory stones at each other.

Pay attention. Presidential campaigns are times to see ourselves in action. Notice the power of words, the choice of words, and pay attention to your responses.

The candidates afford us a view of how we communicate individually and as a nation. Can we find a way to become a more gentle-spirited people?

One would hope that the candidates' intentions—our intentions—are not to hurt each other. Yet, watch as we slip into aggressive behavior, calling each other names, pointing out errors while we attempt to demean each other in subtle and not-so-subtle ways.

I don't know about you, but I find myself cringing when I hear candidates' uttering words meant to undercut the integrity of another candidate. I find myself cringing when news commentators' use words that are unnecessarily critical, words that evoke negative emotional responses, and words that are intended to undermine our perception of a candidate.

Our species thrives on love, affection, kindness, encouragement and appreciation. We wither when the emphasis is on discouragement, judgment, criticism, resentment and blame.

Choosing words that nurture can become a daily practice. Instead of engaging in political banter that leads to conflict, notice when your jaws become tight and your heart begins to race. That's a good time to monitor "sticks and stones."

Disagreements can be an opportunity to enjoy contrasts, to consider new ideas, learn and grow. If we all think the same and agree on everything, life becomes stagnant. Rubbing up against our differences allows us to spark new ideas. Listening with interest, rather than aggressively moving toward dominating another, creates goodwill.

Lively and meaningful discussions are different from those where people talk over each other. Next time you are on the edge of your seat and can hardly wait to have your turn to speak, experiment. Pause before entering the conversation. Notice what happens. Notice who takes your place. Notice where the conversation goes.

Lively and meaningful discussions evolve more deeply when we are willing to experiment with how we participate. Instead of making a statement, ask a question. Instead of giving advice, ask the person, "Have you considered _____?"

Most importantly, we can become aware of our intentions. Before engaging with another, we might ask ourself, "What is my intention?"

When we feel we are right and the other person is wrong, we can practice holding back from saying what we were going to say. If we say something and then realize that we intended our words to hurt another person, it's an opportunity to acknowledge what we did and be courageous enough to apologize for our intents. There is nothing more heart connecting than someone who is willing to be honest, willing to apologize for wanting to be right.

Let sticks and stones be reminders that words do hurt. Let our words be building blocks to becoming more gentle people—more caring toward one another.

■
WHAT'S LOVE GOT TO DO WITH IT?

EVERYONE NEEDS AND WANTS TO BE LOVED.

It is a "universal" need. Valentine's Day comes and goes. The bouquet of roses wilts. The chocolate box is empty, and the candy hearts with messages were eaten by children. Special valentines are hidden away as remembrances for future years when we long to remember "how sweet it was."

There are romantics, those who love to receive love letters and flowers as sweet reminders of love. And there are words of expressing love, often an uncomfortable challenge. Whether you are the romantic or a "tough-it-out" silent type, three simple words can make a heart flutter. "I love you" mends tiffs, softens disappointment, turns sad faces into smiles and encourages communication.

What happens after Valentine's Day? Do you forget the importance of love? How do you express love on an everyday basis? What importance do you place on letting love be known?

In working with Hospice, I saw how important those three words are. I'm not talking about a casual "I Love You." I'm talking about making eye contact. Bring your full attention to that person and speak with sincere intent.

I hear many times, "If only I had told her how much I loved her." Or, "I would give a million dollars to tell him just one more time that I love him." Parents whose children die tragically or unexpectedly or at an age that seems too young, there is a sinking feeling of, "If only I had said 'I love you' more often."

Life doesn't tell us when we will die. Thoughtlessly, we don't like to think today may be our last day. We forget that when a loved one leaves for work, it may be the last time to see him or her, the last opportunity to say, "I Love You."

How often do you to tell your friends how important they are to you? This is a way of saying I Love You. What about Aunt Gracie or Grandpa and Grandma, the ones who think you are the most special person in the world? When did you last say, "I love you"?

Yes, Valentine's Day, anniversaries, and birthdays help us remember to express love. But, if we only remember on that one day, we miss the most important day—today!

Declare every day as Valentine's Day. Look yourself in the mirror every morning. Tell yourself that you love the person you see. Put a red heart in every space of your calendar for a month so you remember to practice expressing love every day.

Commit to taking action: kiss someone, hug someone, tell someone how much you appreciate them. Keep that love-stuff circulating. The more love we keep in circulation, the more currency we have. That means keeping it current!

Smile at a stranger. Tell a child how thoughtful he or she is. Stop by a retirement home and pass out flowers to every person you meet. Pay for a coffee for the person behind you in the drive-thru espresso stand. Spontaneously buy popcorn for a couple of kids at the movies. Offer to walk the neighbor's dog. Tell the postal workers that you appreciate their patience and thoughtful dispositions. Kind words are love seeds that propagate.

What's love got to do with it? Love is contagious. The more you give, the more you receive. Up your ante! Say, "I Love You." Say it again and again. Watch your heart grin.

AWFULIZER OR ENERGIZER

ARE YOU AN AWFULIZER OR AN ENERGIZER? Awfulizer people drain energy. They bring "dark clouds" where people gather. From their point of view, life is bad, and it's getting worse. "The weather is lousy, the stock market is dismal, and the boss is annoying." Awfulizers love to download their whoas—they seem to be optimistically challenged.

The Awfulizer run's rampant with Ya-but's. "Ya-but, I know I won't get that raise. Ya-but, I know my boyfriend doesn't love me. Ya-but, I won't get the job, so why bother applying? Ya-but I'm too old to make changes." Sound familiar? Any ya-but people in your life?

Awfulizers are those who "shoulda, coulda, woulda". "If there were more hours in a day, I woulda finished that project. My car was in the shop, otherwise I coulda helped. I know I shoulda deposited that check, but I ran out of time." Beside this, "I shoulda known better!"

The antithesis of Awfulizer is Energizer. These people exude positive energy. They smile and say hello. They call to check in, and they send thank you notes to express their gratitude.

Energizers take the time to encourage others who face difficult challenges. In the face of despair, Energizers see opportunities in what appears to be hopeless. They have learned and value the skill of turning sour lemons into tasty lemonade.

Who do you know that is an Energizer, that one person that lifts your spirits when you are feeling lonely, exhausted or challenged?

It's truth time. Awfulizer and Energizer reside within each of us. You choose which to express. It's up to you.

There may be a lot of awfulizing going on in the world. It's easy to feel bombarded by news of an awful economy, awful relations between countries, awful condition of healthcare and economy. Awefulness can be convincing if awfulizing is the main focus of your thoughts.

I believe it is our innate nature to want to be happy. There is a saying, "change your thinking, change your life." This teaches us to pay attention to what we focus on. What we focus on determines the level of happiness we experience in life.

Imagine your life lived in a room with windows, but you never open the windows. Your experience of life is stale air. Then one day, someone says, "Hey Joe, why don't you open those windows?" You open the windows and are filled with the sweet taste of fresh air.

Energizers focus their thoughts on positive things—things that make others happy. They support you, and themselves, by choosing to uplift and encourage a deep sense of satisfaction—"fresh air," so to speak.

Fresh air is energizing. There are medical studies that show people who redirect their thoughts can reverse life-threatening illnesses. Awfulizing depletes. Energizing supports growth and wellness. Focus on the goodness in life and find yourself uplifted.

How do you live your life? As a begrudger and moaner? An encourager and appreciator? It's up to you. You get to decide. I guarantee that if you focus on positive thinking, your life will change in meaningful ways. In recovery programs, people practice living one day at a time. Choose, one moment at a time. Energize rather than Awfulize.

It's a practice, moment by moment. Like deciding to get up and go for a walk, you have to get up and move. Know that it takes as much energy to be an Awfulizer as it does to be an Energizer. It's the effect on your life that is different.

What can you do to build up your commitment to being an Energizer? Pat yourself on the back when you get out of bed. Congratulate yourself for being willing to begin again. Decide to pay someone a compliment. And while you're on loving-kindness, call someone or email someone and tell them how much you appreciate their support and friendship.

One of the fastest ways to change Awfulizing is to volunteer. There is something good that comes from giving to others—you get back tenfold! It's the nature of volunteering. If you want to become an Energizer, sign on with Hospice or the Food Bank. Be a reading assistant at the Boys and Girls Club. See how you can make a difference at a homeless shelter or a senior center or a scout troop. What about an animal rescue shelter? Wherever your interest, there is a need for volunteers.

And…if you doubt your ability to refocus your thoughts to become an Energizer, go ahead—practice listening, encouraging, acknowledging and appreciating others. And don't forget to smile! Awfulness diminishes, and the fresh air of positive thinking will energize your life.

Be well. Be happy. Be Energizers.

LAUGH MORE!

TESTING, TESTING. ONE…TWO…THREE…

1. There was a man who entered a local paper's pun contest. He sent in ten different puns hoping at least one would win. Unfortunately, no pun in ten did.

2. One day a man went to see Mozart's tomb. When he got there, the tomb was open and Mozart was sitting there tearing up pieces of paper. The man asked: "What are you doing with all of your great works of music?" Mozart replied, "I'm decomposing!".

3. "Doctor, whenever I drink tea, I have a pain in my eye." The Doctor replies, "Take the spoon out of the cup before you drink."

Okay, did you muster a grin or are you laughing out loud?

I know you *love* that feeling when you laugh. Yes, that exhilarating feeling when you laugh so hard that tears roll down your face, your belly shakes, and you hoot and howl from spontaneous, uproarious laughter. That grand spaciousness where pain and suffering vanish, and for a moment there is nothing but a sense of light-heartedness—a profound sense of well being.

Laughter uplifts! It is documented that laughter releases endorphins into the bloodstream. Released serontonin builds up your psycho-neuro-immunological system. All this shaking from laughter creates internal vibrations that release the stress in your organs. The oxygen level in your blood increases giving you more energy. Blood pressure lowers, and stress diminishes.

Norman Cousins discovered the power of laughter by laughing himself to wellness. In his book, *Anatomy of an Illness as Perceived by the Patient,* he shares that 10 minutes of hearty laughter gave him two or more hours of pain-free sleep every day.

Laughter not only heals illness; it has the power to diminish the most tragic and deep sense of loss. It buoys your spirits when in doubt or when you feel anxious. Comediennes have learned to take these real-life situations and make us laugh at them. They stretch and exaggerate the situation beyond what you thought possible. It's like taking a balloon and filling it further and further. Eventually it pops. This is the nature of humor and laughter. Take a life event... exaggerate it (fill it up to the brim) and you burst into laughter.

Laughter provides a new perspective on any situation. When you learn to laugh at yourself, you admit there is another way of looking at the situation. Instead of focusing on the seriousness of what has happened, you view the experience as laughable. Charlie Chaplain said, "to truly laugh, you must be able to take your pain and play with it."

A willingness to let go of suffering through humor and laughter affords you more social connections—laughter is called social glue. It bonds us to the people we laugh with. A smiling face has more magnetic power than a frowning face.

How can you increase the amount of laughter in your life? Is it possible to feel light-hearted? I encourage you to try several of these suggestions and watch your life change:

- Start a support group specifically for laughing and exhibiting joy!
- Throw a weekly dinner party and ask your guests to bring "funny food"—a chance to get silly and very creative!
- Ask your children or spouse to tickle you every day just to jumpstart laughter.

- Laughing is a "high-impact" internal workout—you burn up 500 calories if you sustain a full-belly laugh for one hour. Think of the benefits!
- Rent comedy movies, watch clips on Facebook and YouTube or listen to CDs containing live comedienne recordings—laugh, laugh, laugh.
- Attempt to be friendlier—just for the fun of it.
- Create a clown brigade and spend one day a week making people smile.
- Search "humor" on the Internet—and laugh away an hour.
- Make a practice of reading funny greeting cards.
- Stand on the street corner blowing bubbles. Smiles will abound and surround you.
- Make up funny holidays and invite your friends to come celebrate them.
- Read the cartoons in magazines and newspapers.
- Become a trendsetter for light-heartedness: Ask your friends to support you in laughing more. Challenge them to join you in setting aside "seriousness".

Now it's up to you.

Have you heard this one? *Mary Poppins moved to California. She became a fortune teller, but didn't read palms or tea leaves. She smells people's breath. That's right, the sign outside reads: Super California Mystic Expert Halitosis.*

Okay, okay, let me try one more. If you aren't grinning after this one, I can recommend a great cream that removes frown lines!

A teenage girl had been talking on the phone for about half an hour, and then she hangs up. Her father says, "That was short. You usually talk for two hours. What happened?" "Wrong number," replies the girl.

YOUR HEART IS NOT A COMMODITY

OKAY FRIENDS, TIME TO TELL THE TRUTH. Raise your hand if you are single, divorced, widowed, partnered or married. Good, we're together.

Now let's see what happens with the next question. How many of you are between forty and eighty, single, and are seeking a loving relationship? Keep your hand up if dating makes you insecure. Or do you stay in a dysfunctional relationship because you fear no one else would be interested?

How many of you worry that you're not attractive, or, who will be there to care for you when you grow old?

You are not alone. Conditions exist that affect how we relate, communicate, and support relationships. We are a consumer-oriented society obsessed with belongings, driven by corporate advertising and mass media marketing.

And guess what? This purchasing of consumables has a flip side called disposables. Take your big-screen TV, or that blazing-fast computer, the designer phone, cars, gadgets, clothes—always something bigger, better, faster or more glitzy. You "have to" upgrade. This behavior spills over into how we see the world and how we manage our relationships. It has everything to do with the gradual erosion of human values.

The human spirit, the soul—call it what you like—knows that belongings have no heart and that the human race needs "heart."

There is a part of us that needs to be valued, appreciated and loved without having to shape ourselves into something we are not. We are a species not to be sampled and discarded—possessed and thrown away, yet we do this. Ouch!

I say "ouch" because consumerism permeates our society. It creates stress, self-criticism, and judgment. Am I beautiful, smart enough, fast enough, rich enough? Do I have the latest and greatest and do I know how to use it? We move too fast. Upgrade, recycle, dispose and impose in cycles that create competition and suspicion of other's intentions.

Online dating replicates thumbing through a product catalog. Pick an item. Sample the goods. When it arrives, if it doesn't sound good, look good, or do what you hoped, you return it. Trade it in for something else.

Books teach you how to market yourself and how to shop for your perfect dot-com match. Professional copywriters try to convince you they can help you stand out in the sea of singles seeking sex, romance, and partnership.

The human heart aches when reduced to buy, sell, trade, or discard. It is not intended to be packaged like a commodity—bought, sold or traded.

What are we doing? Give up the "am I handsome enough, educated enough, thin enough, rich enough, and do I do enough?" Turn your attention to the idea that "you are enough."

Value yourself and others. Transform impatience, criticism, self-righteousness, put-downs, blame, and shame into expressions of loving kindness, thoughtfulness, caring, sharing, accepting, appreciating, and befriending.

Yes, there are wounded hearts and wounded relationships because of consumerism, but you can reclaim your values. You can embrace your human potential. Pay attention to your relationships with friends, family, and your spouse/partner. Heal the dis-ease by noticing the language you use. Witness the times you are impatient, rude or judgmental, then apologize and practice being a more loving person.

Give up rationalizing and making excuses. Tell the truth. Instead of possessing and discarding, grow and encourage. Develop daily practices that sustain and nurture quality relationships. Focus on playful activities. Eat together. Laugh. Engage in meaningful conversation. Tell the truth. Express affection. Comfort each other. Show you care. Make new choices to keep your attention on valuing, appreciating, and cherishing life.

The human heart is sacred. Like a heritage seed, value and nurture yourself in a field of love that produces more of the same.

Remember: You are NOT a commodity. You are a person of "heart"—strong as the oak tree, supple as the willow, lovely as the rose, and brilliant as the stars. Take Gandhi's advice, "Become the change you wish to see."

HELLO...ARE YOU THERE?

"This 'telephone' has too many shortcomings to be seriously considered as a means of communication. The device is inherently of no value to us."

— Western Union internal memo, 1876

WE HAVE OUR SHORTCOMINGS—our limited thinking. Consider today's telephone. Imagine thinking this "device is inherently of no value to us." Compare the 1876 vision with the reality of today's world.

The old-fashioned ring-a-ling of a telephone is now a choice that includes harmonic tones, riffs of Bach and squeaks, squawks, bells and knock-knock-knocks. Where it once hung on your wall or sat on your desk, the telephone tucks in a pocket, a handbag, and is an accessory in your car.

It has become an appendage. We use it whenever and wherever, and without a cellular signal, we whine. Add to this, we invented headphones, earbuds, hands-free, auto dial, iCloud storage, and yes, our phones can photograph, record, play games, and watch live news coverage. This device fills a deep need to communicate—to stay connected.

With the telephone no longer just a phone, technology gives us instant messages and FaceTime. We listen to Podcasts and music and play games. Who would have imagined telephones becoming compasses and maps! We shop and place orders with same-day delivery. Using our fingers to type is replaced with audio dictation transcribing words into instant messages.

This endless wish to stay connected has spawned a whole new language—an abbreviated language of symbols and short-cuts and emojis. The word "what" is replaced by the simple question mark (?). No longer do we say that we laughed out loud. Now it's LOL. But wait, we have grinning emojis—a laughing face with tears rolling from our eyes. And endless variations to express our emotions. Choose a heart symbol to express your mood—red, pink, green, blue, even black. If you are out-of-touch with technology, the once familiar "xoxo" is still recognizable as "kisses and hugs."

Our species naturally explores and discovers. We want to connect with life. Consider that not so long ago, messages took weeks or months by horseback. The invention of the telephone and telegraph moved communication using electronic signals. Today, high-speed, instant access is the norm.

Live images and news from around the world reach us as events unfold. We see celebrations, wars, weather-related disasters and often are overwhelmed—bombarded with real-time news. We move through time zones, into foreign countries with immediate access to what is happening to citizens in every country.

Are we communicating any better than when we sat around an open fire or around the kitchen table? We learn how to use the latest devices, but have we improved our communication skills? Are we listening or are we shouting? Do we move too fast and fail to hear what is said? Do we know how to listen? Instant messaging is one thing. Understanding the message and responding is something else.

Sometimes I long for a great sh-h-h-h of silence. A collective silence when our species turns off every device and listens. Imagine the sound of silence. What does it sound like? One heart beat?

LOVE SICK

"GET OVER IT," YOUR BEST FRIEND SAYS. "Valentine's Day was a week ago, and you didn't get the roses, the lace-trimmed panties or the romantic dinner."

It may be Hallmark's second biggest card-sending holiday, next to Christmas, but whining and weeping won't help you get over being lovesick. Hallmark gets the prize for earnings, and you get it for yearnings.

No vaccines prevent love sickness. I know many of us would rather die than live without the person who made us feel all those lovesick symptoms, but let's put all this in perspective.

When lovesick, we drive others nuts. We take extraordinary measures to dress right, say the right thing and strut our stuff ad nauseam.

We talk about the object of our love as often as possible. What's intoxicating to us becomes toxic to those around us. Everyone seems to end up sick with this thing called love.

Doesn't matter if you are young or old, many yearn to love and be loved. Unfortunately, yearning is not love. It blinds us with infatuation—a state of the mind that overlooks reality. Remember when you convinced yourself, "He can do no wrong. What a guy!" Soon he's on a pedestal. Two years later, you find that the business trips he took were mini-vacations with a lover.

Raise your hand if you have experienced infatuation based on physical appearance. "She's the most beautiful woman I've ever met," you tell a buddy. Yes, and three years later you admit that she isn't in love with you. She loves your money and has manipulated you to her advantage.

Love often comes out of nowhere, hits us alongside the head, and rational thinking fails. Ordinary daily decision-making becomes hindered because we can't think about anything but the new beloved.

No one is immune to the lovesick bug, including the elderly. My grandmother caught "the bug" in her mid-70s. Smitten with a man who courted her with all kinds of sweet endearment, I remember how animated she became. Her skin took on a rosy color and her lips softened. Never think it can't happen to you!

There is another variety that strikes certain men when they reach the age of 50-something. They become love sick at the sight of every 20-year-old woman. This one is interesting because it crosses the boundaries of age.

One problem with this boundary crossing is that it can worry the parents of the 20-year-old girl who is the object of his love. The parents suffer from anxiety and fear. They lose sleep thinking, "How could our daughter consider marrying that old codger?"

But love crosses lines of age just as it crosses lines of society's gender norms. There are plenty of people who get sick when their son becomes lovesick over another family's son. And your daughter announces she is dating Tammy.

Family members are sickened by the news that their Caucasian, Baptist-reared daughter has fallen in love with a brown-skinned, Catholic man from Jamaica. They refuse to meet him. Or, the family who disowns their Chinese son because he is marrying a Latino political activist. "It makes me sick," are words spoken more often than we might imagine, and it's all about what we call love.

What to do? What to do? Love sickness shows up in so many ways over the course of our lives. We promise ourselves we will never fall in love again. But love has a way of showing up when we least expect it and in the most unlikely ways.

If we were to hospitalize ourselves every time we are lovesick, or sick about love, hospitals couldn't provide enough beds. "He broke my heart," you tell the doctor. Unfortunately, researchers haven't found the cure for love sickness or how to repair a broken heart.

We turn our backs on those whose love we disapprove of, yet the power of love never goes away. Love sustains, inspires and nurtures while it makes us vulnerable, foolish, and sick. Love pushes up everything unlike itself. It cannot be possessed. Jealousy, bitterness and mean-spiritedness are attempts to control love.

Love can be fickle. It can last a lifetime—and even beyond a lifetime. French author of Le Petit Prince *(The Little Prince),* Antoine De Saint Exupery expresses beautifully, "Love begins when nothing is looked for in return."

COMPASSION IN A HEARTBEAT

WOULD YOU GIVE YOUR LIFE FOR YOUR CHILD? Yes, in a heartbeat. And how often do you give your heart to another person?

Compassion is that moment when we connect with another—expressing concern and empathy. It's one heartbeat that leads to another.

Is it that simple? Just a heartbeat?

In any moment, we can extend compassion toward others and ourselves. Whether it's at the breakfast table, the office or in a city council meeting, every human interaction opens the possibility of feeling deeply connected.

Everyone has a need to be seen, heard, appreciated, valued and acknowledged. We are alike.

And, our interconnectedness includes suffering. Everyone suffers to various degrees over a lifetime. Sometimes we are tired, overworked, financially strapped, or ill. Sometimes we fail and feel insecure or devastated by a loss. While we may struggle to rise above it or aspire to spiritual realms free of suffering, the human experience includes suffering.

When we are impatient, judgmental and unkind—to others and ourselves—suffering occurs. This creates chaos and amplifies our own suffering. We decide, "I'm not going to suffer alone!"

Others dig themselves into a deep hole setting out to prove that "no one suffers as much as I do."

How can we free ourselves from this suffering?

Admit that we are human is the first step. Accept that every person has, or will, experience suffering teaches us that we are never alone. Someone, somewhere, is experiencing something similar in any given moment of our lives. The day comes when we are in need and appreciate a few heartbeats of compassion.

No one is perfect. Sometimes we act as if we're perfect. In those moments we hide behind a façade, afraid of exposing our humanness, our vulnerabilities, our imperfect weaknesses—and our errors. Forgiving ourselves when we pretend to be perfect is another building block for extending compassion to others and ourselves.

Sometimes we are not completely honest. Times when we are self-serving. And times when we could help someone but don't.

It's easy to accuse others of having serious shortcomings. But, if we want to become compassionate people, we need to turn inward first and ask, "Have I ever done something similar?"

If we admit our shortcomings, we allow ourselves to connect with others and create compassion in a heartbeat.

Millions of people suffer from addictive behavior, and we avoid talking about it, let alone extending compassion.

Addiction is feeling out of control with alcohol, drugs, food, tobacco, gambling, sex, video games, TV surfing, shopping—you name it—and it's rampant in our society. Denial, self-blame and shame keep people addicted.

To admit the truth extends compassion to those addicted, including ourselves. We feel helpless and hopeless. The truth frees us from self-loathing and self-blame. Reach out to spiritual communities for counseling and recovery groups. Courage empowers us to show compassion for others and ourselves along the journey to reclaim our lives.

Sometimes we can't control judging, blaming and criticizing others. It's easy to point fingers toward politicians, public servants and those who appear to have more power than we do. But are we willing to walk in their shoes? Ask yourself, was there a time when I had to make tough decisions? Can I remember when I made mistakes, when I was under pressure and stress? For every question we ask ourselves, we open to the beat of a compassionate heart.

Separate yourself from the issue and the details. Return to person-to-person, heartbeat-to-heartbeat. This is the path to becoming compassionate. Shift from self-serving interests to building healthy families, community, and cooperation. Lead with compassion.

As a tool, the well-known Serenity Prayer can help us: God, grant me the courage to accept the things I cannot change, the courage to change the things I can, and the wisdom to know the difference.

WALK YOUR TALK

MY FAVORITE UNCLE USED TO SAY, "Don't take up smoking, honey," and then pull out another cigarette from his Lucky Strike pack. "Do as I say, not as I do," he'd say, then flip his Zippo lighter and cough as a smoke cloud encircled his head.

Children are influenced by what adults say. I could tell that he enjoyed smoking, yet his words contradicted his actions. As a child, I bought boxes of candy cigarettes and puffed away, imitating my uncle's behavior.

As an adult, I smoked for fifteen years before I found myself telling my daughter not to smoke while I continued to smoke. Then the ah-ha moment: What difference does it make to my daughter if I don't walk my talk?

It's my integrity. Every step I take out of alignment with my integrity, I disappoint others and myself. Integrity is like a carpenter using a plumb line. Align yourself and things come together beautifully.

Take a moment and ask yourself: If I gave myself a report card, what grade do I get for walking my talk?

We hear parents shout, "Will you stop yelling!" An example of "do as I say, not as I do." And we wonder why children don't do what we say!

When we don't walk our talk, we show that we don't respect ourselves enough to practice what we preach. We convey the message that our children, our friends, and our family don't deserve honesty. Or, do we think they're not smart enough to observe our actions don't match our words?

A classic example: Two children are fighting, one hits the other. A parent steps in and swats one child on the rump, saying, "Don't hit!"

What's the message? Don't hit until you're a grown-up?

How can we change our incongruence? First, pause before speaking. Will you follow up on what you say? Do you believe what say and do you live that belief? Then ask yourself, what is my intention?

These simple questions go to the heart of the matter and eliminate mixed messages. Check your intention. For example, if you take a moment before giving advice, you may find you are attempting to change the behavior of another.

Try as we might, we can't change anyone. But, pay attention to your intention and you may uncover self-righteousness and criticism. The "ah yes, I see that I'm putting myself above others," can help us change rather than trying to change another.

I remember a conversation between a married couple. She pointed out that her husband never listens. He attempted to answer. She cut him off with a list of "yes buts."

"Yes but you interrupt too often." "Yes but have no patience." The behavior she was pointing out was something she was unwilling to see in herself.

The adages, "actions speak louder than words" and "practice what you preach," are another way of saying, "walk your talk."

How do we learn to walk our talk? We trip now and then with double standards and unspoken demands we place on others and ourselves. These signposts point to eliminating our own incongruence.

Take a periodic inventory of your beliefs and values. Are they outdated, or even your own? Sometimes we parrot the beliefs of others without realizing they are ingrained family beliefs. Unearthing what is true for you can improve communication between family and friends.

If you expect others to show up for meetings on time, show up on time yourself. Don't start arguments and then wonder why you find yourself arguing. If you say you stand for peace, live peacefully. Is respect important? Then respect others.

Walking your talk demonstrates self-awareness. Relax. Enjoy the walk!

THE ART OF WEIGHING AND MEASURING

HOW DO YOU LIVE A FULL LIFE, find meaning, and deeply appreciate everything that comes your way?

My method is something I call the art of weighing and measuring. It's a lifestyle focused on the awareness of what you're doing and how you're doing it. Simultaneously, you learn to appreciate the value of experiences—from the mundane to the extraordinary.

A good place to begin is by reacquainting yourself with your senses. If you're sitting in a comfy chair, luxuriate in that comfort. If you're sitting on a hardwood chair, how does your bottom feel against something that has no give.

What is the quality of light and the temperature of the room? What sounds do you hear—including your heartbeat. This simple practice opens you to the world of sensory awareness, a wonderful way to explore the art of weighing and measuring.

In any given moment—anywhere—you can pause and practice by asking yourself, "Am I aware of what's happening around me? Am I using my senses?"

You might find it interesting to weigh and measure how often you want to speak. Pause before allowing the words to come out of your mouth. This practice requires you to become aware of opinions, judgments, and your need to give advice. Are you uncomfortable with silence and want to fill the space with idle chatter? Ask yourself, "What happens if I keep my mouth shut? If I say something, is it a contribution or am I intentionally creating conflict?

Weighing and measuring words is an excellent practice for improving relationships. For those who are gregarious and outgoing, refrain from speaking. It helps you notice when your ego gets puffed up—when you need to be right or need to be the center of attention.

For the shy and insecure, weighing and measuring is a practice of observing how quickly you retreat. To assert yourself and express your thoughts through words can balance your tendency to withhold your ideas or beliefs.

Do you weigh and measure your time? Are you aware of how much time you spend on the internet, or how much time you watch TV? Get out a stopwatch and clock yourself for a couple of days. Weighing and measuring how you use your time can be invaluable. It affords you a view of how you spend your precious minutes of every day.

Once you are aware of how you spend your time, you can make new conscious choices. Maybe you scale back time spent on one thing and open up space for other things that are more enriching. You decide which activities improve the quality of your days.

I have a friend who recently joined a sailing club. She doesn't have a boat and has never sailed, but she loves the water, enjoys social contact, and wants to learn sailing. In weighing and measuring, she realized that something was missing from her life. Initiating change, sailing renewed her sense of joy in learning, growing and socializing.

Another friend found that taking time for herself in quiet meditation improved her energy and outlook for the day.

Do you weigh and measure the things you consider drudgery? If you don't enjoy cleaning house and end up powering through all-day sweat marathons, try weighing and measuring. Break housecleaning into manageable pieces—clean one room each day and it is no longer overwhelming.

Learn to re-think drudgery by refocusing and changing your perspective. Instead of complaining, view those tasks as great ways to move your body. Then, cleaning becomes a routine exercise. Go ahead—dance with the broom!

Weigh and measure the time you spend with friends, family and pets. Is it quality time? Do you need to spend more time with your family and do less golfing or playing bridge? Change what you do and see if your spouse is more appreciative or your children more communicative.

These simple evaluations, the daily weighing and measuring, become an art for improving and appreciating the quality of your life. It's a way of learning how to balance things. Work and no play? We know where that leads.

Go ahead, weigh and measure.

WHAT A DAY!

THE PLUMBER WAS TO ARRIVE BY 9:00 a.m. I canceled my dental appointment so I could be home. Did the plumber show up? No. He had an emergency.

In the meantime, my dog coughs-up ghastly looking stuff on the carpet, requiring special spot cleaning. This is only minutes before the auto service center calls to say they found a major problem with my car.

"Do you want the work done?" the mechanic asks. My stomach churns. My heart pounds faster. I search my mind for options and blurt out, "I don't have a choice. Go ahead."

No sooner do I finish that phone call, but the phone rings again. A friend calls to complain about having too much on her plate. All I can say is, "Sounds familiar. Let's get a grip."

By the time we hang up, I hear my email box dinging its reproachful sound. One-hundred sixty-five unread emails!

I feel sorry for myself. "Who cares if I have a bad day?" The thought sends me deeper into a one-person pity-party, already well under way.

I know if I call one of my spiritual friends, I will remember, "it's how you look at it. Change your perspective."

If I phone my astrologically-wise friend, her perspective: "Mercury is retrograde." And, my nurse friend will say, "It's hormonal, Honey. Relax."

Relax? On a day like this? No possibility. Around every corner, something looms to make the last glitch seem like fluff. By now, misery is looking for company.

It occurs to me: Go back to bed. Pull the covers over your head. Save yourself. Tuck up under the warm blankets. Prevent your world from spinning out of control. Out of control? Me? The world? Never.

Yes, I could choose to soak in the bath tub, but I'm a shower person. A warm, relaxing soak would mean breaking a ten-year habit. What's more, I would risk encountering who knows how many dead spiders. Why they choose to die in an unused bathtub baffles me, and I am not in the mood to risk a dead spider scene. With the day going as it is, the notion of confronting spiders, living or dead, is not what I need.

I look at my watch and then at the dog. It is nearly noon. He has that look on his face: "I'm so cute. Will you take me for a walk?"

"Take you for a walk? Can't you see I'm having a bad day?"

His tail wags, hoping it will make a difference. Don't you wonder what your dog thinks? I do.

It dawns on me: This is why dogs chew bones. It's better than chewing off someone's leg when they're having a lousy day.

Thinking about chewing bones makes me realize eating something might reduce my frustration. Yes, food is a great comfort. I open the kitchen cupboard. A box of cereal falls out. I knew I should have secured the top the last time I pulled it out. But here it is, payback—cereal all over the counter! The dog stands there wagging his tail with that grin on his face.

As I collect the noodle-shaped pieces of bran, I glance out the kitchen window to see the lawn grinning. I promised to mow it yesterday and didn't. There it is, staring at me, reminding me of what happened the last time I put off mowing. When ignored, my lawn grows five inches over night.

I glance at the bran, then the dog with his wagging tail, and back to the lawn and decide I will eat a bowl of cereal and fruit. Having breakfast twice in the same day seems like a good idea.

As I tear open the self-closing strip on the frozen blueberry bag, it gives way and pops open. A few rogue blueberries roll onto the white counter, each one leaving a bluish-red trail.

As I top off the cereal and blueberries with a scoop of plain yogurt, the dog's tail wags furiously, oblivious to my plight. I desperately need to get food in my stomach.

As I head for the deck to enjoy sun and fresh air, I remember this is the day I have a column to write. It's due today. "What? Today?"

Good grief! There you have it—what a day!

FORGIVENESS...
IT'S ABOUT YOUR WELL-BEING

ARE YOU RESENTING A FAMILY MEMBER for words spoken at a Thanksgiving dinner? Is there a friend who embarrassed you at a Christmas party, and you won't let go of your anger? Do you begrudge anyone for anything and say, "I won't forgive that person!"

If you think you have to forgive, you are not authentically forgiving. Having-to is a must and is not from your heart—it's you doing something because someone told you to do it.

If you pretend to forgive—acting as if you are no longer angry or resentful—you are negating feelings and not telling the truth. For example, "I forgave him a long time ago. He's a jerk and I don't want him occupying my mind." You say you forgave, but listen to the undercurrent of resentment.

Resentment, blame and anger become dis-ease in relationships and dis-ease in your body. Consider this: Quantum physicists recognize that emotions condense as energy particles. If not expressed, they become lodged within the atoms and molecules of your body.

Stored resentment is a cellular memory. Every time you think of the person or what occurred, that inner "memory" gets activated. Resentment surfaces as a physiological response—muscle tension, perspiration, rapid heartbeat. You mutter, "He's a jerk and always will be a jerk." Or, "She embarrassed me one too many times. I'm not giving in to her again!"

How long do you carry resentment? Are you interested in forgiveness as it relates to your well-being?

Forgiveness effects your health. It frees you from suffering. You and the other person might not become fast-friends, but you can be free of resentment. The unpleasantry that occurred won't change, and it does not mean you will forget what happened. In fact, it is a good thing to remember what happened because experience guides you in making future decisions.

Forgiveness dismantles the negative assessment you have invested. Look at your judgments and the stories you constructed. By repeating the stories in your mind, suffering continues.

What can you do with resentment? Begin by making a forgiveness list. List any person you resent or direct negative energy toward. Beside their name, place a number between 1 and 100—1 represents a small amount of resentment, and 100 is extreme resentment. This list helps increase awareness of current relationships and the intensity of resentment you are carrying. Change begins with awareness!

Now, choose one person from your list and record the facts that happened. Focus ONLY on the facts. For example—It was Christmas morning. The gifts were under the tree. Tom was sitting on the sofa. Tom drank a glass of wine. I was sitting in the blue chair. The children sat on the floor—and so on.

When you finish listing the facts, list your interpretations. For example, Tom was being his usual, lazy-self, boozing it up as he always does. I sat waiting for Tom to get off his duff and start passing out the gifts. It's the same thing every year. I remind him that the kids are anxious to open the gifts, and I need to get dinner in the oven. When I suggested that he start passing out the gifts, he exploded telling me that I control the gift-opening every year. "Why can't you just wait until I'm ready to begin instead of always having it your way!" (Note the attitudes and beliefs and judgments that go into interpretations. It's important to remember that every person in the room will have their own interpretation of what happened.)

Now, examine your thoughts, beliefs, rationalizations, and attitudes you still carry. Notice the importance you place on details of your interpretation. This is how and why you keep the resentment loop operating. The "story" belongs to you. You repeat it numerous times. If you give up "the story," resentment falls away. The other person becomes a person—not someone attached to your whirling story of resentment.

Ask yourself these questions:

1. If I forgive, how will I see this person?
2. If I forgive, what belief will I no longer have?
3. If I forgive, how will I treat this person?

And finally...

4. If I forgive, how will I feel?—calm? peaceful? happy?

This inquiry is helpful in letting go of the "story" that keeps you bound in resentment. Ask yourself questions and your heart opens to the possibility of seeing a different perspective. It's the willingness to "walk in the shoes of another person"—seeing with compassionate eyes instead of eyes filled with judgment and thoughts that keep you telling the old story.

Let go of the story. Let go of the dis-ease. Forgive and be free.

WHAT'S YOUR INTENTION?

"WHY DO I SUFFER?" Now ask, "What were my intentions?"

Examining intentions turns on lights, affording you to see how you live your life. Do you intend to be generous or tight-fisted? Do you intend to be honest or deceitful? Do you intend to love or be fearful?

Before you take action, ask, "What is my intention?" This inquiry guides you to the truth of what you are about to do. It helps hone your integrity—living from self-respect and respect for others.

Sounds simple, yet looking at your intentions can be challenging. It requires noticing when you skirt the truth, make up excuses, and justify your actions

Intent #1: A friend cancels on you—backs out on something you looked forward to doing together. Next time you see your friend, you act aloof.

Friend says, "Is something wrong?"

"No, nothing's wrong."

"Great. Let's have coffee."

You respond, "I'm busy."

Stop! Ask yourself, "What is my intention?" You may discover a harbor of disappointment. Rather than feel like a 7-year-old who wants to get even, you avoid the truth. And the truth? "You didn't play with me, so I won't play with you!"

If you are grinning, think of times you or someone else has acted out with a plan of "getting even."

Intent #2: You are a teenager who wants to go to a baseball game but can't afford the ticket. Every day for two weeks, you drop hints to your dad. One evening, your dad explodes, "Damn it, why don't you ask me for the money!"

Now you are dealing with a blast of anger. Rewind the scene. Ask yourself, "What was my intention? Did I expect Dad to be a mind-reader?"

The answer? "I wanted dad to pay for my ticket without me having to ask." Being direct and honest may avoid angry outbursts from a dad who feels manipulated.

Intent #3: A month ago, a friend borrowed $10. Today, that friend asks you to go for dinner. At the restaurant, instead of addressing the $10 debt, you order an expensive entrée plus a glass of wine. When the check comes, you say, "Let's split it." Your friend responds, "I want to pay for what I ordered."

You are now steaming and stewing. Your intention was to resolve the debt indirectly and earn a small amount of interest on your $10 loan. Now you have added fuel to your own fire. Look at your intentions and you may learn to value integrity and communication.

Intent #4: You pick up speed to get to an available parking space. You see another person headed for the same space. You accelerate and zip in, avoiding eye contact.

As you leave your car, the grandmotherly woman challenges you, "Are you happy that you bullied your way into that space?"

"What do you mean?" You respond as if innocent.

Rewind! What was your intention? Truth-told, you intended to out-maneuver the old woman. Now, you want to cover up your embarrassment for your bully actions. In addition, you don't feel like apologizing.

Question your intentions and you will find the level of truth from which you live your life.

Do you give someone a back rub because you want one in return? Are you fixing a fabulous meal to sooth unkind words spoken earlier in the day? Do you watch endless hours of TV to avoid interacting with your family? What prevents you from telling the truth?

What is your intention? Asking that question brings awareness. It has the power of shifting you from playing small to walking tall.

Go ahead, ask yourself, "what is my intention?"

SELF-TALK...
THE KEY TO FEELING TERRIFIC

CONSIDER SELF-TALK. Nattering, "do this and don't do that," is a familiar critical voice that produces diminished self-worth.

Now, consider resistance, your unwillingness to change or do things differently.

Your potential is extraordinary, yet you ignore how powerful you are. You long to avoid complaining. You want to grin, laugh and be included. If only you could change.

You fall into a less-than-worthy attitude. "If only I were healthy. If only I was friendly. If only I was beautiful, talented and artistic."

Compare yourself and you lessen your worth. It's a self-perpetuating cycle. The message is, "I'm not okay," and sure enough, you end up acting out those words. It's easy to dig yourself into dark spaces—find yourself helpless, hopeless, and unworthy. Life is challenging enough without criticizing yourself.

The antidote to negative self-talk is positive self-talk. It's that simple. Each time you criticize yourself, interrupt the pattern and say kind things. "I am a good person, healthy and happy. I am loved and love others."

Positive self-talk is as powerful as negative self-talk. Know it or not, you learned what you think with repetitive self-talk.

Yes, a parent or teacher or friend may have judged you or said something demeaning. When it occurred more than once, you decided it was true. The glitch? You added your own self-talk to deepen the untruth.

Children learn to be seen and not heard. "Be quiet unless we speak to you." When the child starts school and a teacher says "sh-h-h," this child is influenced by an internalized a message: "Be quiet." When this child becomes an adult this person hesitates to speak. "Why bother speaking when no one will listen?" This is demeaning self-talk that reinforces a negative self-image.

Everything you think impacts the quality of your life. "I am weak and fragile" makes you emotionally and physically vulnerable. "No one loves me" keeps people at bay. "I'm stupid" inhibits your ability to learn.

Affirm inner strength—beyond your wildest imagination—and resources keep you strong and healthy.

Marianne Williamson wrote a lovely piece used by Nelson Mandela in his inaugural speech. Two of the lines speak to self-perception: "Our deepest fear is not that we are inadequate. Our deepest fear is that we are powerful beyond measure."

We have inner resources to change and grow and be everything we want to be—love and be loved. Enjoy health and happiness. Be generous and joyful—"powerful beyond measure."

If you start today and make a daily routine to speak positive self-talk, you will become healthier, happier, and stronger.

Get up in the morning. Greet yourself in the mirror with enthusiasm—"Good morning, best friend. I love you. You are a healthy, happy person." Practice for thirty days.

Caution: You may become an inspiration to others!

■
PRACTICE GRATITUDE

WHEN THANKSGIVING COMES AROUND, we think of gratitude —two important words: Thank you. They allow us to connect heart to heart.

Gratitude is the healthiest antidote to suffering and negative nattering. It lifts the human spirit.

Imagine grumbling, complaining and blaming infused with gratitude. That means listening to the complainer and notice how often you complain. Then, infuse your awareness with gratitude. Experience a whole new quality that transforms these repetitive behaviors.

Have I've gone mad? Einstein said we can't solve problems using the same means used to create them. We need to shift, move to higher ground, change our perspective to come up with new ideas. So consider the possibilities of this new approach: Use gratitude.

When someone rants that he's right, you're wrong and who knows what's really going on, ask yourself, "How many times do I do this?" Then, let this be your opportunity to stop ranting and pointing fingers. Be grateful to see yourself in the actions of another. Appreciate choice.

Practice using every negative, energy-depleting thought as a springboard to shift into gratitude? You don't even have to specify why you are grateful, just grin with gratitude for staying out of negative thinking.

Imagine the person who repeatedly antagonizes you, baits you into an argument. You recognize the internal agitation that's being set off as your stomach says, "Here we go again."

This is a great opportunity to remember the times you've jumped in and ended up sorry for the escalation. Pause, shift and focus on gratitude. Instead of entering the familiar, consider other points of view.

Gratitude frees and eases anger, pretense, self-righteousness and the sword of indignation. "Thanks for giving me the opportunity to see how I tend to defend myself."

We go through bruising elections. Maybe your candidate won and maybe not. Instead of whining and stewing, imagine looking through the eyes of gratitude. Be grateful for the right to vote. Thank the candidate for inspiring you to become more involved. Your opponent helped energize you to take a stand. You climbed out of your recliner and campaigned for your beliefs.

And, don't overlook every day thank you's. Phone or email a friend with a simple, "Thanks for being my friend."

Consider the waitress, the nurse and the housekeeper who do everything they can to make you happy, comfortable and satisfied. Thank you, thank you, thank you.

Remember a time when someone motioned for you to take a parking place or let you go ahead in line? Appreciate these ordinary generosities by extending them to others.

Life gives and life takes away. Gratitude through sickness and death can be challenging. Yet, expressing relief that a loved one went swiftly, or appreciating that you were able to talk one last time are honest means of sharing your experience. Thanking those who showed up for the life celebration is an expression of your appreciation. Gratitude nurtures us.

Gratitude is a choice. There are people who welcome everything. They find the silver lining in a flat tire. "I'm grateful I had my cell phone with me," or "What a blessing that a Good Samaritan stopped to help," or "I'm fortunate that having to stop spared me from a traffic accident."

The guy who shouts, "Hurry, you jerk," may be your guide to patience. Thank him for reminding you to reduce your speed.

Sometimes we win and sometimes we lose. A gracious winner and a gracious loser can express gratitude—gratitude for the opportunity to play.

We make mistakes. We win, we lose, we say things we wish we hadn't said. To accept our humanness softens the heart. Seeing beyond the need to be right, or the need to win, affords us an opportunity to say thank you to all concerned.

And, when disappointed in humanity, we can restore our hearts by turning to nature. Walk in a blustery wind, view snow-capped mountains, listen to rushing rivers, smell fertile farm land and your heart can't help but say, "thank you, thank you, thank you."

Even broken hearts signal an opportunity to be grateful for loving and being loved.

Share this book with someone who has extended gratitude to you. Thank them for inspiring you to "pay it forward."

AUTUMN'S LESSON: IMPERMANENCE

GREEN LEAVES, ONCE SECURE ON SUMMER TREES, now vulnerable. It won't be long before wind shakes them loose, causing their final descent to earth. They yield to impermanence.

A rusty nail, its shiny finish succumbs to time and moisture. It, too, reminds me that nails are impermanent.

My grandfather's hair, once thick and brown, turned gray when he was 35. Eventually it fell out revealing baldness that forced him to face impermanence.

Although we know everything dies out, wears out, falls out, impermanence is a challenge for each of us. It raises issues of insecurity and helplessness. We feel out of control.

Intellectually, we may accept impermanence, yet emotionally we resist. We squirm and look the other way, hoping that we won't have to change, hoping that the change that is occurring will not radically shatter our sense of security.

Our seemingly secure relationships continually change. One day we get along; the next day we are at odds. One day our global community seems fragile; the next day news of hope gives rise to renewed strength.

We move into the season of autumn that holds a fixed place on our calendar, yet what is the lesson of impermanence? Are we learning to appreciate the bite of chilly mornings or the importance of appreciating the warmth of summer that becomes a memory?

Life has its way, reminding us there is a limit to "having it our way." Yet, we resist. We purchase products that will prevent sagging skin and deep-set wrinkles. We swallow pills to relieve emotional discomfort, to lessen our pain, to enhance our sexual prowess. We cling to the idea of eternal youth and avoid appreciating the beauty of aging.

My friends, you can't keep it all together. This lesson of impermanence pops up in all aspects of life. The flow of money, the weight of your body, the temperature of the room, the ground beneath your feet all fluctuate. And, isn't it interesting to notice how well you manage, or don't manage, endless change?

The impermanence of life challenges us deeply when death comes knocking. Overwhelming grief is not uncommon when facing impermanence of this living flesh and impermanence of relationships that we wish could last forever.

How can we accept, rather than resist, impermanence? I suggest spending time outdoors, experiencing and appreciating nature. Nature teaches us to be with what is and provides one lesson after another.

It affords us the opportunity to see that we can choose how we respond to impermanence. Learning to let go and learning to tolerate uncertainty are options when we are willing to accept the changing seasons, the shifting course of a river, hills that become rockslides, and migrating geese honking encouragement from above. Patterns of life are endlessly changing. Why do we resist simple lessons that afford us deep learning?

Be aware of the obvious, and the subtle—whether it is your body, your home, your village, or your global community. Moment-by-moment everything is changing. I encourage you to see life through the eyes of wonder and awe.

I encourage you to come up with reminders like, "Don't push the river." This simple reminder can ease you into acceptance of the transitory nature of life. One cannot push the river—plain and simple!

Accepting impermanence can free you from suffering, complaining, and spending energy in useless arguments with nature. Be willing to experience the expansiveness between summer and autumn, contraction and expansion, night and day. Accept the power of both concepts without being pulled in either direction—without having to choose between one or the other. Learn to appreciate the quality of impermanence. There is no need to choose.

Awareness of this sort IS the discovery of peace and freedom without struggle. The lines we draw to define conservative or liberal, rich or poor, large or small are imaginary lines that we can easily imagine as having no function whatsoever.

Ask yourself, "What am I thinking?" Then imagine the freedom of no longer needing to draw lines, no longer needing to choose sides. Stretch, reach, and open yourself to a greater potential.

I encourage you to deeply consider the importance of impermanence.

■
WHAT'S LOVE GOT TO DO WITH IT?

EVERYONE NEEDS AND WANTS TO BE LOVED. It's one of those "universals".

Valentine days come and go. Bouquets of roses wilt. The chocolate box is empty, and we chew the little hearts with messages. How sweet love is.

There are the romantics—those who love to receive love letters and flowers and sweet reminders that mean, "I love you." And non-romantics may find this whole business of expressing love a very uncomfortable issue.

Whether you are the courageous, romantic or shy person, speak three words—I love you—to make any heart flutter.

What fills that universal need for love? How do you express your love? What importance do you place on giving and receiving love?

In doing Hospice work, and experiencing the death of a beloved on over one occasion, I realize how important it is to tell people how much I care. I'm not talking a casual "I Love You." Take your time. Look into a person's eyes, or at least, bring your full attention to speak with great intent. Everyone expresses with individual uniqueness. Sometimes it's a pat on the back. Sometimes it's an act of kindness.

I have heard many times, "if only I had told her how much I loved her," or, "I wish I had told him one more time how much

I loved him." We can't know for sure when we will die. Today may be the last day, the last opportunity to say, "I Love You."

Tell your friends how important they are. Share with co-workers qualities you appreciate in them. Do you express gratitude and share joyfilled memories with your brother or sister? When did you last say thank you to a friend for being your friend? Put a red heart in every space of your calendar for a month so you practice expressing love from day to day.

Once a year, Valentine's Day helps us remember to express love and appreciation. One day leaves 364 other days to express love. Start by looking at yourself in the mirror. Tell yourself every morning you love the person you see.

Think about things that plant seeds of love. Visit a retirement home and pass out flowers to every person you meet as you walk the hallway. Pay for a coffee for the person behind you in the drive-thru espresso stand. Buy popcorn for two kids at the movies. Surprise anyone with an act of kindness. Offer to walk the neighbor's dog. Tell the postal worker you appreciate his patience and courteous disposition.

Love is contagious. The more you give, the more you receive. Up your ante! Say it again and again and again: I Love You.

■

WHAT'S WITH THE "VIBES"?

...OR DOESN'T THAT QUESTION MEAN ANYTHING TO YOU? I grew up during the '50s and '60s where "she has good vibes" was a meaningful communication to most people.

Good vibes produce a positive emotional reaction. When someone comes into the room crying, that person is emitting sad or disturbed vibes. How do you respond? With calm, compassion? Or do you become fearful?

Are you aware of your vibes? They come in the form of words, actions, facial, verbal, and body expressions, and subtle energies that can be miniscule, yet they are present.

Do the corners of your lips turn downward, or are they turned upward more often than not? An upward turn is more friendly. Smiles are signs of welcome, trust, and interest.

Is your brow furrowed and your eyebrows skewed into a scowl? Go ahead, look in the mirror. What do you see? Next time you are at your favorite cafe, notice the facial expressions in the person sitting across from you. Is that person's face saying, "I'm angry" or "I'm stressed" or "I'm relaxed"?

Notice hand gestures. What vibes do you sense? If you are waiting at a traffic light and the person in the next car has fingers tapping on the steering wheel, are they vibes of impatience? Or is that person keeping beat to the music?

Handshakes have vibes too. Do you shake with a vise grip? Is this a person who lacks confidence and compensates by breaking your hand? What do sweaty hands show? Nervous? Frightened? Or, just finished running a mile?

Are knees bobbing? What's the vibe? If music is playing, the person is keeping rhythm to the beat. At the office, leg bobbing could show tension, impatience or boredom.

Notice a person who slouches. Lazy? Bored? Or, "leave me alone"? What is your emotional response to that person? Hm-m-m…interesting to consider, yes?

When you are talking with someone and they divert their eyes—what message do you translate? Are they saying, "I'm not interested in what you're saying," or "I have a short attention span," or "You're taking up precious time."

People slam doors. What is your response? Do you assume they are angry or frustrated? In contrast, other people tip-toe and give off vibes of insecurity, fear, low self-esteem, and uncertainty.

What does the tone of your voice show? This is one I especially know because when I get excited, impatient, or frustrated, my voice raises two octaves. I find myself not only raising from alto to soprano, but I become louder and the rhythm of my speech quickens.

Pay attention. Check out your heart beat and breathing patterns. When you become angry, anxious, or frustrated, does your heart beat faster and your breathing more shallow. If you pay attention to these two body functions, you can develop self-monitoring which can help you regulate feelings of hostility and impatience. Awareness affords you to choose your vibes: shift from nervous aggression to peace and calm.

Have you sensed vibes that caused you doubt or fear or a sense of being unsafe? Sometimes vibes are based in an environment. For example, a vacant lot where trash and old cars have accumulated, or a dark alley that smells of urine, or a hot unventilated room. Each of these settings may evoke an uncomfortable atmosphere.

Animals give off vibes too. You have a "sense" of caution around dogs that are growling or snarling or barking—a caution warning. A wagging tail gives you vibes of feeling welcomed, approved, and loved.

To develop your skills for reading the vibes of others, I encourage you to first trust your gut. If tense, ask the person if they are angry, or excited, or sad, or anxious. By asking, you can confirm your "read." The more you practice, the more skilled you become in reading vibes. This is a skill called trusting-your-intuition.

Do you gravitate to people who are calm, happy, giving, playful, honest and friendly? Do they bring out those qualities in you?

When you sit with your arms crossed tight, your head slumped and your jaw tight, and your spouse asks, "Is something wrong", and you answer, "Everything is fine," do you think he or she believes you?

Body language, tone of voice, and choice of words are indicators of disposition. Become a vibe-sensitive parent, student, employer, employee, friend and lover. You never know the power of being a vibe-reader until you practice checking out your own vibes.

Be well. Be aware.

■
DON'T FALL IN THE HOLE

YOUR FRIEND WALKS ALONG the street and falls into a hole. "How could that happen," he asks pulling himself up and out.

Next morning, he walks the same street and falls into the same hole. "What! Why do I keep falling into this hole?"

The following morning, your freind is on the same street and notices a warning sign: Caution, Hole Ahead. He scratches his head, "How long has that sign been there?"

He continues walking, looking back at the sign. Good grief! He falls into the hole again. As he crawls out, he is angry and frustrated. "Why does this keep happening to me?!"

Next morning, your friend approaches the warning sign. He stops. "I want to avoid this hole." He turns back and goes down a different street. How simple life can be! Watch for the warning signs and you avoid falling into holes.

Let's look at a simple warning sign. You and your sister-in-law struggle every year over who will host the 4th of July party. And, every year you fall into the same hole—the same argument.

You run into her at the market. She mentions she has three new friends she wants to invite to this year's 4th of July party. Your stomach turns into knots: Warning, Warning!

Instead of heeding the warning, you assume it's your turn to host the party. You have plenty of chairs so three extra people is no problem. You respond, "I'll set up three more lawn chairs."

She looks at you with disdain. "You hosted last year. It's my turn. Besides, they are my friends." Thud! You both fall into the hole.

How could you avoid this annual bantering? First, pay attention to the warning sign when your stomach knots. Commend yourself for your observation! You won't take that street again. Instead of falling into the familiar argument hole, you ask yourself, "How can I go around this?" The point is, find a different approach.

A grin spreads across your face catching your sister-in-law off-guard. She was prepared to fall in the hole with you, but rather than argue, your smile directed her to a different path.

She says, "Since we have hosted for years, let's have someone else host this year." Not only do you both avoid falling into conflict, you veered onto a new path. It's no longer "your way" or "her way." You are facing new possibilities.

Pay attention. Old habits are warning signs. They blind us and cause us to fall into conflict and pain.

This takes practice, but, when you look for warning signs where you repeat behavior that causes you pain, consider a new direction.

What is a "hole" you often fall into? Maybe you can't say no to a fast-food drive-through? Your car veers in and you have no control? Or, what about the money you spend on gas because you're the nice guy who always drives. Yes, falling into a hole includes many patterns you aren't aware of, yet you say, "Ouch! There I go again!"

Sometimes your choice of friends might not support your highest good. That person phones you and asks you to join in the fun. The "fun" is one of those holes you fall into and don't enjoy having to climb out again and again.

Make a list for yourself. What unconscious behaviors or habits cause you to fall into a hole and wonder why you are there again.

Name it. Once you name the truth, you admit that you see yourself in that "hole." That's where you begin choosing a different path. One day at a time. Change your route. Associate with different people. It's good to notice which side of the street you choose as your path from here to there. Don't fall in the hole!

"Life can be sweet on the sunny side of the street."

■

BECOMING YOUR OWN BEST FRIEND

ARE YOU YOUR OWN BEST FRIEND? Do you treat yourself with kindness. Are you willing to forgive yourself?

Sometimes I hear people say the meanest things about themselves. "Boy, am I dumb!" or "That was a stupid thing I just said," or "I can't stand how I look," or "I wish I was a nicer person." So many self-inflicted judgments and resentments!

And if we aren't judging, are we blaming ourselves for past transgressions that occurred years ago? These negative litanies reinforce self-loathing. No wonder people don't spend quality time with themselves. They believe they are unlikeable.

Where is your self-worth? And, why do you criticize yourself? Even some of us appear to have strong public personas but are self-critical.

Let's sort this out. If you give yourself negative messages throughout the day, you are not your own best friend. Being a "bestie" with yourself requires paying attention to self-talk.

Do you tell yourself your neighbor doesn't give a hoot about you? Have you convinced yourself you are lazy, no good, unkind, and worthless? Hm-m-m…what a heavy feeling.

There is hope! Get thee to a mental laundromat! Yes, it's time to cleanout that mental chatter that keeps you from seeing how loveable you are. I know, I know. You argue that you don't need your ego pumped up, but I'm not talking artificial inflation. I'm talking how-to-learn to like yourself. Become your own best friend. Clean up your negative self-criticism.

It begins with simple acts of kindness directed toward yourself. Yes, you! Start the day with a new practice. Commit to greeting the day with thanksgiving and enthusiasm. Talk to yourself with gentle words. For example…"Good morning _____ (fill in your name). I love you. Today is a great day."

That sounds more pleasant than grumbling and dreading another day. At first this might seem uncomfortable. Do it anyway. With practice, you will relax and enjoy greeting yourself and welcoming a new day.

Once out of bed, stand in front of a mirror. Look yourself straight in the eyes, and tell yourself, "You're terrific!" If old self-talk rears its ugly head, like, "Me terrific? I don't think so," listen and repeat, "I AM a terrific person."

To become your own best friend is to change the habitual negative self-talk. Don't give up! Notice negative thoughts and replace them with positive statements. You are planting "new seeds." It takes time for seeds to germinate. Patience is essential to new growth!

Commit to yourself to do this exercise every day for one month. And, make the commitment to someone else you trust. Here are instructions for cultivating positive changes in your life…

Write one positive phrase on a small card or slip of paper. You will need only four cards—one phrase for each week of the month. Read the Week 1 phrase out loud every hour for seven days. Then, write a different phrase for Week 2, Week 3 and Week 4. Or, use my suggested phrases below. Remember: Read the card every hour on the hour—preferably out loud, but sometimes out loud isn't proper. Then read silently.

This process is a jumpstart to becoming your own best friend. Here are four suggested phrases to repeat.

Week 1: I am my best friend. I treat myself with kindness.

Week 2: I forgive myself for wrongs I have done and accept myself unconditionally.

Week 3: I let go of judging and criticizing myself and others.

Week 4: I am my best friend. I extend kindness to myself and others.

Practice this process for one month. You have nothing to lose and everything to gain. Enjoy befriending YOU!

HOLY DUNG

DUNG HOLY? I think it's a topic we need to discuss.

Some of us are up to our knees in it, and it doesn't smell purdee. Yet, in order to get out of the dung, we have to face it. How we do that is what we're going to talk about. It's about perspective, perspective, perspective.

If you have an aversion to the smelly stuff of life, you probably keep it at arms length. Acting like it isn't there does not work when it comes to death and dying. Like the elephant in the middle of the room, its a good thing to talk about it.

My guess is that most of us recognize there are a lot of things we don't like to face. Things we don't like to talk about because we disagree, or we have radically different beliefs and don't believe talking about it makes any difference.

What things do you not like to talk about? Politics? The economy? Healthcare? Religion? Your "goofy" uncle? Death and dying?

The things we don't want to talk about are usually things that "clog the plumbing," prevent life from flowing with ease and grace.

What clogs the pipeline of communication for you and your family? Who do you refuse to talk to? Who has offended you, cheated you? Who's feet are stuck in the muck?

When we look at life as a "system" and the system needs to flow, most of us have been guilty more than once at being a clog in the plumbing. We refuse to move, to give in, to change course. And the longer we remain stuck in our position, the stinkier things get. Sounds like families and politics.

Yes, politics and relational plumbing happen whether we are interested or not. Some align themselves with this uncle or that uncle, with a favorite aunt or a tight-fisted aunt, or a ruthless stepmother versus a biological mother. It's all about connections and the flow of life.

There is hope. Rather than sit around and complain, it's wise to admit there are many Holy Dung experiences in life. Looking at them from many perspectives is a creative process that can change the plumbing.

Consider fruit that falls from a tree, or grass that is mowed and composted along with food scraped from dinner plates—it all becomes compost, transformed into nutrients for new life

If you were to look through creative eyes and focus on transforming current perspectives, outdated beliefs, and immense challenges, what would be the most awesome transformation you can imagine…so awesome that your spontaneous response is, "Holy Dung!"

One of my beloved aunts died sitting on the toilet first thing in the morning. I never imagined dying on a toilet, doing "your business" and the "Maker" taps you on the shoulder, "It's time."

Knowing this aunt and her spontaneous laughter, I imagine she said, "Holy Dung!" as she slipped to the floor with a smile on her face.

A TIME FOR THANKS

IT'S TIME FOR THANKS. And, how often do you put off expressing gratitude and appreciation only to find the opportunity lost? Maybe you overlooked the mechanic in the repair shop whom you have trusted for years. When you discover he's left the job, you realize how much you valued his talent and you never thanked him.

For me, it's easy to take for granted the people I greet at the park when I walk my dog. Many I don't know by first name, yet they are people I enjoy meeting and sharing brief comments—usually relating to our dogs or the weather or the beauty of the park. I appreciate their presence, yet what prevents me from thanking them for being a regular part of my life?

Consider the friendly clerk at the post office or the grocery store or the pharmacy or library. Do you say "thank you for your good service?" And, do you let your neighbors know that you appreciate them as good neighbors?

Consider friends and family who live a thousand miles away. How often do you express your appreciation?

People die. People move away. And it's too late—you've missed an opportunity. Your heart aches with regret. Voila! It's time to express gratitude to those you love. Time to give thanks for nature's respite and beauty. And time to give thanks for the freedom and opportunities we enjoy in our lives.

As we face local, national and global challenges, focused gratitude is essential to our well being. Appreciate small things, things that inspire and sustain you. Value your connections with others, with nature. These are daily opportunities to live in gratitude.

Gratitude dissipates fear and reduces anxiety. With an attitude of gratitude, begin the day with prayerful thoughts of thanks for being alive. Turn to your beloved partner, family and friends and say, "Thanks for being here."

Hug your children. Remind them they are blessings in your life. Pet your pets. Befriend the elderly. Do random acts of kindness leaving behind a silent trail of goodwill.

Take time to gaze at the stars and smell autumn leaves as they become mulch. Behold the wonder of the sun peeking through the morning mist and wave as you watch an eagle soar. Let your ears tingle with pleasure at the sound of the river as it winds along its stone-lined bed.

What in your life inspires gratitude? Good health? Peace of mind? A job that satisfies you? Do you focus on small things every day? Do you express gratitude for things that fill your heart with joy?

Instead of complaining, express appreciation. Speak positive words with a loving voice. See everything as a blessing—even when it comes disguised in unpleasant trappings.

It's easy to give thanks for what we perceive useful, but sustainable gratitude comes with a willingness to be thankful for any fortune—large or small. Gratitude is a state of being.

Extend kindness and service as a way of saying thanks—a way to give back and stay connected. Volunteer as a tutor, an aid for the elderly, or join a trail maintenance team. Seeing a need and filling it makes you part of a larger circle of giving and receiving. At the end of each day, consider where you've been, whom you've met, and how much you enjoyed the day. Give a thousand thanks for every breath you take. Gratitude is the sweetest of all—once, twice, a thousand times.

My thanks to you for reading this book.

■

ABOUT THE AUTHOR

Ruth dreamed of experiencing cultures beyond her Swiss, small-town upbringing. In 1969, she hitch-hiked from Wisconsin to San Francisco. Civil rights, womens' rights, gay rights, and equal rights have been the focus of her lifestyle since that time.

Ruth earned a Masters Degree in Psychology, a Doctorate Degree in Religious Studies, and owned a graphic design business in San Francisco for ten years, and another in Sausalito for ten years. She also taught typography to students at the Academy of Art in San Francisco.

• • •

Ruth and her partner moved from Mill Valley to the Olympic Peninsula in 1999 to semi-retire. Her partner died a year later. Where she grieved deeply, a community of newly found friends helped her settle into a new lifestyle in Sequim.

Moved by their kindness, she wrote an essay on grieving and submitted it to the *Sequim Gazette,* offering it as comfort to others during the holidays. The editor of the *Gazette,* Sue Ellen Riesau, phoned and asked if she would like to be a columnist.

Ruth never imagined writing monthly columns for the next seven years, but it turned out to be a meaningful entré to the community. In addition to the *Sequim Gazette,* she wrote a quarterly column for *Living on the Peninsula.*

Living alone and grieving the loss of her partner, she decided to write one-line daily inspirations and email them to friends in California. Those friends passed the inspiration on to other friends and within a year, Ruth had over a thousand people from around the country subcribing to her free morning email service. Three-hundred-sixty-five days a year, for seven years she wrote and emailed the inspiration!

One of the subscribers sent her an email saying, "You should publish a book of these inspirations." And so, she did. Having written over 2000 one-line inspirations it wasn't hard to select 365 for publication. The book, *Inspiration to Open Your Heart, Awaken Your Mind and Touch Your Soul* is still selling as a special gift book.

• • •

In 2018, she became interested in publishing a collection of Haiku and original mandala drawings. This was a meditative process that became a unique hardbound, 4-color book, *Haiku & Mandala: The Wedding of Ancient Art*. It is available at WideAwakePublishing.com.

Ruth's passion for writing includes hosting writing groups—prose and poetry. Her poetry has been published in the *WA129 Poets of Washington Anthology* (selected by State Poet Laureate Tod Marshall, 2017), *Last Wednesday Poetry Anthology* (2013 & 2019), *Cirque* (Vol. 8.1 and 10.1), *Tide Pools* (2016, 2018), *Art Inspires Poetry*, Craven Arts Council & Gallery, N.C. (2015, 2016, 2018), *Bainbridge Poetry Corners, Hummingbird* (2018); *Frog Pond Journal* (2017, 2019); *Modern Haiku* (2019), *Spontaneous Writing* (2018); and *In The Words of Olympic Peninsula Authors (Vol. 1)*. In addition, she was published in *Storyborne* (2020).

Ruth loves life on the Olympic Peninsula enjoying time with her daughter, granddaughter, rescued-dog and her many writerly, bridge-playing, walking and bird-loving friends.

CURRENT BOOKS BY RUTH MARCUS...

Inspiration to Open Your Heart, Awaken Your Mind and Touch Your Soul

Haiku & Mandala: The Wedding of Ancient Art

Good Grief: Fifty-Eight Ways to Manage Your Life

AVAILABLE AT
WideAwakePublishing.com
Port Book & News in Port Angeles, WA
IngramSpark
Amazon

The author, Ruth Marcus, can be reached at writersonthespit.com

CPSIA information can be obtained
at www.ICGtesting.com
Printed in the USA
LVHW090809050720
659748LV00007B/607